D1196733

HOME OWNERSHIP

HOME OWNERSHIP
Martin Pawley

THE ARCHITECTURAL PRESS: LONDON

First published in 1978 by The Architectural Press Ltd: London

ISBN: 0 85139 304 7

Printed in Great Britain by
by W & J Mackay Limited, Chatham

Contents

Acknowledgements

A book of this kind is necessarily, in a sense, a work of collaboration. As any writer of history (however untrained) must, I have drawn freely on the labours of others whose names are listed in the bibliography.

Great as the debt is which I owe to all these authors—who are of course in no sense responsible for any errors I may have made in interpreting their work—I must single out one volume without which the present book would have been impossible. Of the two standard histories of the building society movement, E. J. Cleary's *The Building Society Movement* (Elek 1965) is the most informed, objective and comprehensive. Its achievement may one day be equalled, but it would be almost impossible to excel.

Responsibility for the conclusions drawn here is not shared, but I am grateful for the insights afforded me by conversations or correspondence with the following individuals: Norman Griggs (General Secretary, the Building Societies Association); Mark Boléat (Under Secretary, the Building Societies Association); Oliver Cox (Shankland/Cox Partnership) and Bruce Douglas Mann MP.

Introduction

In 1918, a year within the living memory of our grandparents if not our parents, less than 10 out of every 100 homes in England and Wales were owned by the families living in them. Out of a population of 38 million less than 14,000 were council tenants. Out of 8 million dwellings more than 7 million were owned by private landlords whose tenants paid a weekly or monthly rent. The building societies, 1300 separate savings and loans establishments, boasted total assets of less than £70 million and only 600,000 shareholders and borrowers.

Today 55 out of every 100 homes in England and Wales belong to the families occupying them. Out of a population 10 millions greater there are 5 million council tenants. Out of 17 million dwellings only 2½ million still belong to private landlords. The building societies, their number reduced by more than two thirds, have nonetheless grown into mighty financial institutions whose total assets rival those of the banks and dominate any other repository of savings—their value in 1977 exceeding £30,000 million. Their total membership, shareholders and borrowers combined, now embraces nearly 20 million persons.

This massive change can truly be described as a revolution: perhaps the greatest triumph of possessive individualism in a century whose progress in many other areas of social organisation has been in the direction of collectivisation and public ownership. Home owners today are figures of far greater political and economic importance than private landlords ever were: their combined voting power not only determines the housing policy of all governments, but settles the outcome of all general elections: the rising value of their homes not only underpins the whole structure of consumer credit, but by extrapolation supports consumer society itself. In a manner which few people understand our entire way of life has come to be secured upon a form of tenure which sixty years ago barely existed.

But in a way that bare existence poses a problem; for though numerically unimportant until after the Great War, home ownership has a history so long that any attempt to describe its meteoric growth confronts from the outset the difficulty of where to begin. It would no doubt be possible to encompass the story in a narrative concentrating on the gazumping boom of 1971–73 when the author's own interest was first aroused, for in that mad period of frenzied buying all the essential elements of owner occupation were laid bare, up to and including the possibly catastrophic consequences of its universal pursuit. But the boom that peaked in the autumn of 1972 began much earlier than 1971: its origins can be traced back over twenty years to the fall of the 1951 Labour government, the last British administration to have espoused rental as the dominant form of tenure. Yet to start in 1951 would be to ignore the impetus given to house purchase by the decline of private rental; itself dating back to the introduction of rent control during the Great War. Rent control is a logical starting point, but it too leaves many strands of meaning extending back into the past, notably in the impact of public health regulations on the cost of building for rent during the 19th century, and in the history of the building society movement.

The building societies provide an alternative vehicle for the whole story. These institutions, of overwhelming importance in the mechanism of house purchase, have a chequered and unstable history extending back to the early years of the Industrial Revolution; while their claimed antecedents, the land buyers' societies, have a recorded existence in the first half of the 17th century. But in their early years the building societies drew heavily on the political privileges attaching to freehold tenure, a legal status drawn from the complex of Feudal rights and duties over property whose origins antedate the Norman conquest. Furthermore the mechanisms of mortgate and rental, like freehold, existed in Roman times, and were codified by the jurists Justinian and Gaius: the first in the 5th century and the second three hundred years earlier. The book of *Ecclesiasticus*, dating from the 3rd century BC, contains the baleful warning that "He who builds his house with other men's money is like one who gathers stones for his own burial;" while two hundred years before that the repudiation of mortgage debts in Athens formed part of the reforms of Solon. Perhaps a full history of home ownership would need to reach back to the clay tablets of Babylon and Assyria in the British Museum, which record land and property purchases two thousand years before the Christian calendar begins—a time when private property, together with coinage, the merchant class, and the institution of slavery ushered in the recognisable historical world.

Each of these possible starting points is authentic because property is universal and timeless and its usages lean heavily on precedent and custom. Yet common sense alone dictates the irrelevance of archaeology and ancient documents to the owner occupier of the late 20th century. This anxious figure, studying property pages, balancing car-port against loft conversion against de luxe kitchen in the game of maximising resale value, seems hardly to be the descendant of the Victorian wicked landlord, the 18th-century squire, or the 15th-century knight. Indeed only ironically can he be compared to the notorious Marcus Livinius Crassus, surnamed *Dives* (the rich), who in the 1st century BC improved houses and resold them—after first buying them from those in fear of fire or collapse in the inner city of ancient Rome.

Compared to the property owners of history we might be tempted to suppose that today's owner occupier is hardly a property owner at all. In contrast to the great estates of the past, his property is rarely handed on from father to son and indeed on average remains in his hands for only five or six years before being exchanged for something better. The size of his possession too leaves something to be desired; both dwelling and plot of land being so small that the poorest yeoman of the Feudal era disposed of greater estates. Furthermore the triumph of the flexible interest mortgage means that his wealth is dependent on the vagaries of interest rates and employment: his home only being a castle to the extent that his credit card is a shield. Yet even this uncertainty has historical parallels: the Feudal knight or farmer enjoyed rights over his fiefdom only so long as his landlord could (with his compulsory aid) defend it himself. During the Wars of the Roses (a struggle for supremacy in England between the rival aristocratic houses of York and Lancaster which took place during the 15th century) numerous estates were confiscated and bestowed on others, only to be confiscated again according to the ebb and flow of advantage during the struggle. At one stage under Henry VI the once vast royal lands, a source of wealth and patronage, were reduced to a value of £5,000 by attempts to buy loyalty. Like the modern mortgage holder the medieval land-owner had no absolute title to his property, only certain rights which a run of adverse circumstances could remove altogether.

Home ownership today, like land ownership in history, is a right to wealth or, more correctly, in the standard economic definition of the word property enunciated by Henry Clay in 1916, a right to the exclusive use of wealth; the prize offered by society to induce people to compete. Notwithstanding his hanker-chief-sized plot of land and unambitious dwelling, the contemporary owner-occupier more than matches up to the Feudal monarch in the matter of property value.

Indeed one strange aspect of the increasing value of the owner-occupied dwelling is to be found in the fact that neither size nor age nor original place in the social hierarchy is of the slightest importance. Not only do mews cottages in major cities, once inhabited by horses and stable lads, now house Members of Parliament; but their country cousins have come up in the world too. In one case recounted by John Woodforde, a cottage in Oxfordshire, grimly distinguished by the story that a tenant, his wife and nine children died there of hunger just before the Great War, came, only 50 years later, to boast a Jaguar at the door and high status as a weekend retreat. Of course the tragic occupants of 1914 had not owned the cottage, but it would have made little difference if they had, for as late as 1950 such dwellings could be bought in pairs for under £150. The difference between then and now lies not so much in the vastly increased demand for ownership as in the change in meaning it has repeatedly undergone in a world the 1914 tenant missed; though in relation to the long history of freehold tenure, by a tiny margin.

The Oxfordshire tragedy illuminates the problem of the starting point very clearly. To begin this book with the gazumping years (even though it conceptually began at that time) would be to wrestle with loose ends leading back into a recent history crying out to be described in some detail. And yet to start only seventy years ago is to venture into a world whose realities of starvation, poverty and disease already belong to an unknowable past.

The second problem in a book of this kind is also inevitable. It is that it will be interpreted simply as an attack upon the building societies—which it is not. The building societies do not exist to solve the housing problems of the nation and cannot fairly be blamed for failing to do so, but this fact is not widely understood, and in part the societies' image-building in recent years is to blame. Massive advertising makes it difficult for the layman to take an objective view of their activities, but this is not the whole reason. As even the summary of the movement's history contained in this book makes clear, there have been frequent and important changes in the role and scope of the societies ever since their birth; and these changes have culminated in the transformation which has become apparent since the gazumping boom.

Ever since the introduction of permanent building societies with professional managers in the 1840s the strategy of the movement has been to maximise growth, and it is this growth rather than home ownership itself which has repeatedly been restrained and canalised by Acts of Parliament in the wake of excesses of various kinds. It is true, as the societies claim, that their association with the growth of home ownership extends back over two hundred years, but by far the longest portion of this history coincided with the decline of owner-occupation in the century before 1918. Even if we take the view that the history of the building societies as we know them only dates from the foundation of the Building Societies Protection Association in 1870, then still their adjustment to private rental as the dominant form of tenure has been of longer duration than their commitment to home ownership. In 1899 they fought the Small Houses (Acquisition of Ownership) Bill which for the first time made local authority mortgages available for house purchase. In 1906 they resisted the Housing of the Working Classes Amendment Bill which would have enabled them to borrow money from the government for subsequent lending to house buyers. In 1915 they denounced the introduction of Rent Control as "The gravest act of injustice ever inflicted by the British Parliament" and thereafter protested its repeated extension; even though this one emergency measure made possible the great home-ownership boom on which they eventually rose to their present prominence. As late as 1944 their Association's Reconstruction Committee advocated the creation of chains of housing societies to build dwellings for private rental in the post-war years. Despite growth during the 1930s they remained uncertain about the true potential of home ownership until well into the 1950s—by which time its tide had become all but irreversible. Only then did they become its champions, and then only within very restricted limits.

It is perfectly correct to argue that no lending institution can be expected to solve the technical and political problems of home ownership in addition to providing the finance for it; but such an argument ignores the extent to which the building societies have come to monopolise access to owner-occupation even as massive investment and increasing economic advantages make it more desirable than ever before. If the building societies today do not wish to be held responsible for a situation in which the over-whelming majority of households in other tenures desire to be owner-occupiers even though with mathematical inevitability a diminishing number of them can afford to be, then they should be able to point to some other means by which this goal can be achieved. That no such alternative exists may not be the wish of the leaders of the building society movement, but it is undoubtedly the result of their present pattern of operations. Not only do the societies operate as a cartel in the matter of interest rates, criteria for lending and so on, but the sheer economic power of the investment in rising value that they hold stands in the way of any alternative method which might be devised to extend home ownership at lower cost to more people.

Thus when I conclude that the pattern of owner speculation which first came into prominence during the gazumping boom of 1971–73 is destructive of the realisation of the now widespread desire for owner-occupation, this is not because I hold the building societies to be wholly responsible for it, but because I consider that their involvement in the process obliges them to think very carefully about the possible consequences of the next great advance of home ownership. It would after all be ironic if the triumph of private ownership led to the nationalisation of the building societies by a Labour government: as ironic as would be the sale by their opponents of five million council houses.

Faringdon
January 1978

Part One
Crime of the Century

1 Freehold and Rent

"Never since the beginning of time was there, that we read or hear of, so intensely self-conscious a society. Our whole relations to the universe and to our fellow man have become an inquiry, a doubt; nothing will go on of its own accord, and do its functions quietly; but all things must be probed into, the work of man's world be anatomically studied. Alas, anatomically studied that it may be medically aided! Till at length indeed we have come to such a pass, that except in this same *medicine*, with its artifices and appliances, few can so much as imagine any strength or hope to remain for us. The whole life of society must now be carried on by drugs: doctor after doctor appears with his nostrum, of Cooperative Societies, Universal Suffrage, Cottage-and-Cow systems, repression of population, Vote by Ballot."

Thomas Carlyle *Characteristics* 1831

From the end of Roman colonization until the Great War, the land laws of England passed through only two major stages of evolution. The first of these stages, ending with the Civil War and the execution of Charles I, is generally characterised as Feudal: the second, while retaining much of the vocabulary of Feudal organisation, clearly embodied changes in the balance of wealth and power brought about by the Industrial Revolution.

In the early Feudal stage, which incorporated some elements of the Roman system, land was held either on a form of tenancy from a sovereign prince, whose title depended on the continued performance of services; or reserved to the state under the title of Folk Land. The tenancy or fief carried with it an express grant of jurisdiction, civil and criminal, over under-tenants and all persons dwelling within the fiefdom. With the passage of time it assumed a more permanent character, becoming first a lifelong tenancy and later descendible in the collateral as well as the direct line. In England, after the Norman conquest, the whole of the land assigned to ownership in this way was divided into about sixty-thousand knight's fiefs; and the tenant of each of these was obliged to serve in war at his own expense for forty days on any occasion in which his services were required. Women who had acquired fiefdoms were obliged to send substitutes under the same terms; as were the clergy, persons holding public office, and men over the age of sixty. In addition to the knight's fief, which was also called frank-tenement (after the Latin *liberum tenementum* or freeholder), there existed a form of tenure known as free-socage. Socagers held title to lands in return for the performance of farm service in the lord's fields and were not required for the more noble duties of military service. Both frank-tenement and free-socage are antecedent terms to the modern freehold, amounting in Feudal times to an upper and lower class of fiefdom.

The latter stages of the Feudal era were marked by a steady increase in the rights and powers of the freeholders, and a diminution in their duties. Under the original system the lord or sovereign was entitled to numerous payments in addition to the major charge of service in war. A large payment, called a relief, was made by every new freeholder upon assumption of the fief; the land itself reverted to the landlord when the tenant left no heir, and was forfeit to him in the event of treason or felony; further payments had to be made if permission was given for subinfeudation, the division of the land to create smaller fiefs. The freeholders themselves enjoyed considerable privileges; in general their lands were not forfeit to creditors until late in the 19th century, even though the 13th-century statute of Acton Burnel permitted the seizure of chattels and forfeiture of land until its income had discharged the debt. Furthermore the fiefdom's grant of jurisdiction, which came to be exercised by all freeholders by vote in the county court, formed the basis of the later franchise for the election of members of parliament. The county court franchise itself was severely limited by a statute of 1430 which stipulated that only the holders of land to the value of forty shillings would henceforth enjoy this privilege; but this act nevertheless had the effect of establishing the connection between freehold property and political power which was not finally removed until the Reform Act of 1884.

With the death of Oliver Cromwell and the restoration of King Charles II in 1660, the Feudal system was officially dismantled;

having ceased to operate as a source of revenue during the civil war. The Court of Wards, which had for centuries adjudicated in matters of fief and escuage, had been disbanded in 1645 and with the execution of the king the pinnacle of the Feudal pyramid disappeared. Charles II agreed to forego the royal income from wardships, liveries, primer-seisins, values, fines, homage and escuage in favour of a pension of £100,000 a year; the first of the payments made to royalty under what was to become the civil list. At the same time all holders of frank-tenement were in effect reduced to the status of socagers, with their duty of service replaced by an agreement to pay taxes determined by the government.

The disappearance of the head of the ancient and intricate Feudal structure of land and property ownership left the body, with its network of obligations, rents and truck payments largely intact. Almost immediately the larger landowners began expanding their estates by taking possession of land which under Feudal usage had been held in common by freemen, small farmers and craftsmen, who made up the bulk of the rural population. This process of land enclosure culminated in the reign of George III when, under pressure of demand for agricultural produce generated by the war with Napoleon, over three million common acres were absorbed into private estates; it did not finally cease until the latter part of the 19th century, by which time it had become inextricably involved with the major political and demographic changes brought about by the Industrial Revolution.

It was the aggrandisement of the large estates, and the pauperization of the small freeholders and yeomen which it caused, that first changed the popular view of the landlord from a kind of reverence to a politically radicalised hatred. Not only did the old Feudal franchise deal unfairly with the new industrial towns; which were for the most part built on leasehold land without charters and without political representation; but the long struggle against Free Trade after 1815, fought by the landowners in order to maintain agricultural prices against foreign competition, succeeded in uniting the rural poor with the new urban proletariat in a powerful political combination. The Great Reform Bill of 1832, which redistributed parliamentary constituencies in favour of the new industrial urban centres, was their first major victory; followed in 1846 by the repeal of the Corn

Laws and the achievement of free trade. In the years that followed the franchise was progressively extended from freehold into leasehold and finally, by the Reform Act of 1884, to all householders irrespective of tenure. Thus the political power of the rent payers steadily offset the freehold rights of the landowners; threatening the eventual end of the landlord class even before the dramatic impact of the two world wars. There were however two sides to the way in which the concept of rent was applied in Victorian times.

In the Feudal sense the term rent derives from the Latin *reddita* to render unto. In medieval times it was generally used to describe the mass of payments and duties required of a tenementer or socager in return for his rights over the land held by him. As we have seen these payments were replaced for freeholders at the Restoration by a general liability to taxation; but for tenants or non-freeholders they continued in addition to taxation in the form of weekly, monthly, quarterly or annual payments for the use of property, principally housing. At the height of the Industrial Revolution most of the new industrial workers were tenants "at will" paying a weekly rent for a tenure terminable without notice by either side.

With the development of commerce, banking and scientific agriculture efforts began to be made to develop an objective means of calculating the precise value of rent, and in consequence the term assumed a second and more specific meaning.

The first widely accepted law of rent was laid down by the economist David Ricardo in 1815. According to him the word could be interpreted as the annual value of the powers of production inherent in the soil: hence different rents reflected different levels of productivity in different areas of farmland, the base line being determined by the productivity of the poorest soil still thought worthy of cultivation. As can be gathered from this description, Ricardo's law of rent was originally applied only to agriculture, then believed to possess an unique efficiency which enabled it to generate a *produit net* or rent; but with the enormous development of the national economy during the remainder of the century it was rapidly applied more widely. It is in fact a useful tool to analyse the progressive failure of the free market rental system in housing under the pressure of industrialisation.

"If the demand for agricultural produce, as shown by the price obtainable, be such as to make it worthwhile to cultivate soils of low productiveness, on which therefore the crop is raised at the highest cost, all land on which the cost of production is less must yield a surplus value which, in proportion as competition is free, falls to the landlord, and constitutes normal or economic rent. It is evident that this rent must increase as cultivation is forced down to inferior soils under pressure of demand and consequent increase of price. Conversely anything which tends to equalise the productiveness of the different tracts of land supplying the same market, either by cheapening carriage or improving agriculture, tends to reduce rent."

This explanation of the operations of Ricardo's law is drawn from Professor F. A. Walker's *Land and its Rent* (London 1883), a standard textbook of the period. From it the reader can readily understand that the law's application to industrial production was very simple, requiring only the replacement of the variable productiveness of different soils by different standards of management, machinery, buildings and so on above the lowest economic level of productivity. By another substitution of terms, Ricardo's law can also be applied to variations in the rent attracted by different dwellings in different locations; but here the specific social conditions of the 19th century intervene in the sense that no base line in the form of a no-rent dwelling existed. In this sense there is another way in which Ricardo's law can be used, and that is in relation to overcrowding.

In the six hundred years which separate the Norman conquest from the first scholarly attempt to determine the population of England and Wales at the end of the 17th century, the number of inhabitants probably increased fivefold to $5\frac{1}{2}$ million. Yet in the 19th century alone population practically quadrupled, from an 1801 census figure of $9\frac{1}{4}$ million to $32\frac{1}{2}$ million in 1901. By comparison the seventy years between 1901 and 1971 have seen the smallest population increase since the 17th century. This massive population increase, which coincided with the enormous demographic changes brought about by rural land enclosures and the growth of manufacturing industry, could not fail to overwhelm the pre-industrial housing process.

During the early phase of the industrial revolution manufacture was extremely labour intensive. At the same time the absence of public transport limited the distance over which workers could travel to and from their employment. In consequence massive demand for worker's housing developed within walking distance of mills, mines and factories. Under a free market economy this naturally suggested high-density housing, closely packed and densely occupied; but here the limited technique and marginal capitalisation of the construction industry imposed certain limitations.[1] Two- and three-storey terraced cottages, derived from rural models, were erected in large numbers, packed as closely together as possible, frequently back to back and always overcrowded. This was the market solution to massive housing need in unprecedented conditions.

Unfortunately the free market solution to the industrial worker's housing problem proved to be a major cause of the Victorian public health problem. Successive epidemics of typhus and cholera (combined with a high incidence of tuberculosis) swept through the densely packed industrial slums and the nerve of the ruling class broke under the strain. Where Malthusian logic might have argued that disease would eventually solve the problem of overcrowding in its own unpleasant way; the spectacle of merchants, industrialists, aristocrats and even members of the royal family being carried off by sickness bred in the slums forced the enactment of legislation laying down standards for sewage, drainage, water supply and ventilation: the economic effect of which was to increase the production cost of new housing enorm-

---

[1]The matter of construction cost and limiting technique is often over-looked in relation to Victorian rent levels. The rural lifestyle of peasants and labourers migrating to the new industrial towns had in no way prepared them for the payment of rent, no matter how small. Prior to the great land enclosures paupers, farm labourers, weavers and yeomen had frequently built their own cottages from mud, sticks and straw, with old barrels for windows and floors made from a mixture of rammed earth and horse manure. Located on roadsides or common land, with no drainage or water supply, the material cost of these dwellings was virtually nil and the labour cost never calculated. Compared to this even a back-to-back was highly sophisticated and a tenement of scarcely conceivable cost and complexity. The additional costs created by public health regulations merely worsened the problem of obtaining rents related to actual building costs without overcrowding.

ously. In an exact parallel with Ricardo's "less productive land" the consequence of building to lower densities was an increase in production costs and a reduction in rent: building for the largest area of demand rapidly became unprofitable.

The limitations of Ricardo's law could nowhere be clearer than in the matter of building costs. In so far as a free market existed, which is to say in so far as health standards were not enforced and overcrowding was uncontrolled, the solution to mounting demand clearly lay in higher and higher densities. In purely economic terms the cheaper the dwelling and the more persons it housed, the higher the "productiveness" of the housing process. But once the first of numerous public health requirements had made their appearance it was no longer possible to match demand by increasing density; and as a result far less "productive" housing was built, so that costs and rents continued to rise with little effective restraint until by the turn of the century the need for public subsidy in one form or another was widely accepted.[1]

With the benefit of hindsight we now know that given the irreversibility of population growth and industrial expansion (by 1870 it was calculated that no less than 40% of the world's industrial production was taking place in Britain) there was no answer to the Victorian housing problem; only a choice of political strategies with which to confront it. The strategies available were three, and between them they have written the history of housing policy ever since.

The first was simply repudiation; to abandon public health and all other restraints upon the free market and thereby return to a market density and a market rent. Paradoxically this stance enjoyed some support amongst both opponents and advocates of public expenditure. As late as 1855, after six major cholera and typhus epidemics in thirty years, *The Times* still favoured "taking a chance" with disease rather than being "bullied" into health; while the related principle of simply dividing the amount of housing available by the number of families who needed it was

[1]Fred Berry (*Housing: The Great British Failure* London 1974) notes that building for rental was in severe decline for some time before the Rent Control Act of 1915. Investment moved drastically from the construction of housing to productive industry throughout the latter part of the 19th century and annual completions fell from 150,000 in 1903 to less than 50,000 in 1913.

advocated by Friedrich Engels (*The Housing Question* 1886) and briefly pursued as housing policy by the Bolsheviks immediately after the revolution of 1917.

The second strategy was suggested by the development of industry and technology itself. Accept population growth, it argued, and accept all the implications of industrialisation, for in the end technology will find ways to solve all the problems created by both and will furthermore create new wealth in the process. There was and is much to be said for this view provided technology is understood in its widest sense. In the course of the 19th century the development of the railways drastically expanded the distance which the average worker could be expected to travel to and from his job, and thus greatly reduced the pressure on inner city areas; a process taken even further by the motor car in the present century. At the same time developments in building technology, in engineering and design, made possible a far more efficient high-density building process than had ever been contemplated before. The use of iron and steel and concrete revolutionised structural possibilities, and the potential of prefabrication suggested unprecedentedly rapid construction. An entire technical specification for healthy, high-density housing within manageable distance of employment had been written well before the turn of the century; and in truth much was built by development companies and charitable trusts in the years leading up to the First World War. Unfortunately the scale of the problem dwarfed these efforts and the legendary achievements of the Victorian engineers found no analogue in free-market housing for the poor.

The problem with any such strategy at that time was that widespread poverty and low public expenditure ensured that it could never connect with the largest and most urgent area of demand: the poor could not pay market rents, and the under-capitalised, fragmented construction industry could not achieve the productivity necessary to bring market rents down. While industries like ship building and the railways attracted their own growth capital, the construction industry continually failed to make the leap into an organised industrial process. Industrialised housing, destined to be a creature of promise for the next one hundred years, failed to follow on the heels of such feats of prefabrication as the Crystal Palace of 1851.

Instead a third strategy was born; the strategy of the managed economy, by which means wealth would be drawn from the community as a whole by taxation and redirected towards those evils of exploitation, poverty and disease which the free market seemed unable to eradicate. Initially at least, arguments for public expenditure of this kind tended to be advanced on the basis of economy; Edwin Chadwick's famous report on sanitary conditions in 1838 stressed that any such expenditure would be preventive and would save money in the long run; but later principles of social justice were advanced on their own account.

The three major political strategies hammered out under the demographic impact of 19th century population explosion and industrial boom have enjoyed a long life. They have, over the last century, claimed credit for each other's achievements and evaded responsibility for their own failures to such an extent that today politics, language and legislation have so interwoven them that only a dense and abstract tapestry is visible: a tapestry in which strands coloured "free market" prove on investigation to emanate from bobbins labelled "technological innovation" and panels entitled "public sector achievement" in fact stand upon frames clearly marked "free enterprise."

This much having been said no one should doubt that the birth and growth of the public sector represented the major achievement of the advocates of public expenditure in the field of housing. The third strategy led in Britain to the creation of a national housing administration controlled by the Ministry of Health and acting through more than one thousand local authorities; each of which was empowered to finance the construction of any housing necessary for the maintenance of civilised standards of life. In the fullness of time this administration came to be responsible for one third of all the dwellings in the United Kingdom. The birth of the council house was not however the only answer to the problem of enabling poor people to live in expensive houses. Long before forty-year exchequer subsidies and penny rates were ever drafted into the financing of house construction, the lowest level of the free market itself had contrived to invent a smaller and simpler form of collective finance: a form which in the same fifty years required by the public sector to gain control of one third of all housing; itself made possible the private ownership of more than half. This innovation was the building society.

2 The Coming of the Building Societies

"We do not want government interference, Government patronage or Government regulation. All we ask is to be set free from the difficulties occasioned by blundering legislation, by perverse Government administration in past years, and by the maze of subtle and confused legal decisions based upon such blundering legislation and perverse administration . . ."

The Building Societies' Gazette 1872

The building societies, like the public schools, have always enjoyed the unfair advantage of having appeared suddenly upon the stage of history, and thereafter claimed long traditions. Though their present importance as financial institutions and arbiters of home ownership is of comparatively recent date, they have, by claiming the paternity of such radical organisations as the Norfolk Land Buyers' Society, constructed for themselves a history extending back to the 17th century. This much is pure revisionism: the truth is that the name building society, which has been in constant use since the last quarter of the 18th century, has at different times meant different institutions operating on different principles with different aims in view. With disconcerting regularity the common building society practices of one period have been proscribed in the next; so much so that the role and scope of the institutions trading under that name today would scarcely be recognised by the pioneers of the movement.

For these and other reasons it is important to survey the chequered career of the building societies before the Great War, in the aftermath of which home ownership first became a mass phenomenon. It was during the 19th century that the societies rose from humble beginnings to a dangerous eminence, from which they tumbled only to recover with a form of organisation so strong and flexible that it made possible their present power. The century of the rent payer was also the century in which the institutions of home ownership learned their business.

The true origins of the building society movement lie in the simple principle of deferred expenditure enshrined in the operations of the Friendly Societies; self-help organisations descended from the Medieval guilds which sprang up all over rural England in the last half of the 18th century. The oldest society now on the register in England is the Bottesford Friendly Society, founded in 1747, while the earliest summary of their purpose is contained in the preamble to a bill for compulsory old-age pensions[1] thrown out by the House of Lords in 1773.

The early Friendly Societies, like the Trades Unions, depended on the collection of regular contributions from a limited membership. They generally operated from public houses whose proprietors sponsored them as a means of increasing their custom, and the sporadic and incomplete records of their activities which exist suggest that there was a high rate of failure from the very beginning. Societies existed for the payment of allowances in periods of unemployment and old age; for the payment of burial charges, and as simple savings banks. Some of them were sponsored by philanthropists among the local gentry, some by clergymen and some by companies such as the railways and mines; but most were small, local organisations in competition with one another for the same clientele, a circumstance which frequently led to abuses.

Despite an alarming record of failures Friendly Societies gained strength throughout the 19th century. Statutes designed to regulate their activities were passed in 1793, 1819 and 1829 (the last requiring an examination of their rules by a barrister) and again in 1834 and 1846 (when the office of Registrar of Friendly Societies was created): in 1855 a further statute required

[1]This strangely anachronistic proposition noted that "Whereas it often happens that persons engaged as journeymen in manufactures and handicraft trades, and, likewise, household servants, labourers and divers other persons, get more money as the wages ... of their service than is sufficient for their present maintenance, and might easily if they were so minded, lay by out of their said gettings a sufficient sum to provide for . . . their old age. And whereas it would be highly useful both to the said persons themselves and to the nation in general that they should endeavour to make such provision." Quoted in B. Kirkman Gray, *A History of English Philanthropy* London 1905.

government certification, but still the catalogue of failures continued. In 1870 the then Registrar, Mr Tidd Pratt, announced that of 23,000 Societies then in existence, not twenty were actuarially solvent: which is to say that if all their members had paid into them everything they were contracted to pay, and all had taken out all they were entitled to receive, the result would have been a deficit. The Manchester Unity of Oddfellows, a Society operating on a national scale, when submitted to this test revealed a deficit of more than £1,300,000. As a result of these revelations a Royal Commission was appointed. The Friendly Societies Act of 1874 was the result of this investigation which, notwithstanding much evidence as to the unreliability and inadequate accounting procedures of the societies, generally found in their favour in the interests of the thrift and frugality they were supposed to inculcate. The Act required the appointment of an overseeing chief registrar and the adoption of uniform accounting procedures, the effect of which was to stimulate more rapid growth still. By 1885 it was calculated that four million out of the ten million working men in Britain belonged to a Friendly Society of one kind or another and the total assets of all societies rose to £2 million by the same year. The incidence of failure was much reduced, but its effects continued: in 1881, 4000 of the paupers in England had been members of Friendly Societies which had failed; 1000 of them had paid subscriptions for more than twenty years.

In 1896 a Friendly Societies Act was passed which rationalised the division of the movement into two branches; one part having grown rapidly from the burial societies into the expanding field of life insurance; the other concentrating on social welfare insurance of one kind or another. The role of the Friendly Societies in the administration of the National Health Insurance Act of 1911 and the Unemployment Insurance Act of 1920 reflected their great power and influence at the time, as on both occasions the Liberal government was opposed to their involvement. By 1920 the entire movement consisted of 28,000 societies with seven million members and total assets of about £140 million, almost double those of the building societies: a relationship which was to dramatically reverse within twelve years.

The early building societies can best be described as Friendly Societies of a particular type. Like their parent organisations some were spontaneous creations of the working class and some philanthropic exercises in self-help sponsorship.[1] In both cases they ran the risks of failure that attend all voluntary enterprises. The important thing was that in their earliest stage of development they were genuinely involved with *building*, and thus for a time at least, lived up to the expectations implicit in their name. In the late 18th and early 19th centuries they had no depositors or investors and did not purchase existing houses. Instead they financed small-scale house building in the same way as the Friendly Societies financed health or retirement insurance; by the collection of subscriptions in public houses. Unlike the Friendly Societies though, the building societies tended to be an urban phenomenon, associated with the enormous expansion of manufacturing towns under the impact of the Industrial Revolution.

A typical society of the early period might consist of twenty people who jointly composed and endorsed articles of procedure or rules which would govern their activities. This fixed membership contracted to pay by regular instalments for a fixed number of shares of an agreed value. As the elected treasurer accumulated funds from these payments periodic ballots were held, the winners of which received share money, generally sufficient to commence building themselves a house. Upon completion of the house the deeds were given to the trustees of the society as surety for continued payment until the loan was repaid and each of the original members had received the sum to which he was entitled.

Since there was clearly a risk of default in these proceedings,

---

[1] The working-class origins of the building societies and their parent friendly societies are often claimed but seldom proven. Kirkman Gray (*op cit*) notes of the latter that ". . . societies afforded no training school for democracy; on the contrary the maintenance of the poor in a subordinate position was far from being an unimportant part of the aim of those who founded them. The charitable school bank, provident club, or friendly society was for the poor, but was not started or managed by them; it was under the control of the well-to-do."

E. J. Cleary in *The Building Society Movement* London 1965, offers a brief analysis of the social background of the members of some early building societies and concludes ". . . the building societies were not wholly working class in their origins. From the first the lower middle classes were well represented in their membership . . . The fact that the Droylesdon Society (1792) collected subscriptions quarterly scarcely suggests that its members were weekly paid workers."

either on the part of the treasurer or of any member who had received money from the fund, the rules contained penal clauses relating to deliquencies of various kinds. The legal standing of these clauses, which often required the payment of fines as well as interest on delayed subscriptions and sums advanced, had not been determined by the Friendly Societies Act of 1793 and all legislation recognising the building societies lay far in the future at the turn of the 18th century. Thus it is significant that the earliest record of a building society in London[1] takes the form of a law report on a case heard in 1812 which for the first time established a legal precedent for the enforcement of the penal clauses.

Pratt v *Hutchinson* concerned the claim of the Greenwich Union building society that two of its members had disposed of shares in a manner not provided for by the articles of agreement, and were seriously in arrears with their monthly subscriptions. The facts of the case were not much in doubt, but the delinquent members invoked in their defence the South Sea Bubble Act of 1720, claiming that since the raising of sums of money by small subscription to build houses was one of the speculations which had called forth the Bubble Act, the Greenwich Society itself should be declared a public nuisance and grievance and the debt voided. They further claimed that the building society practice of awarding exclusive building rights to certain tradesmen amounted to a restraint of trade.

Neither of these interesting arguments was answered by the court, which found for the plaintiff (Pratt, the treasurer of the society) without further investigating the matter; but both the charge of speculation and the question of relationships with building companies were to be raised again in the future.

About 250 building societies were launched between 1775 and 1825, and their number had increased to nearly one thousand by 1836 when the first Building Societies Act was passed by parliament. Of the number launched in the first fifty years about one

[1]Societies arrived in London some time after they had gained a hold on provincial towns and cities. Undoubtedly Birmingham, with no corporation or guild restrictions, was the first town where building societies were formed on any scale; thereafter they spread to other parts of the Midlands and the North. Societies did not appear in London in numbers until the 1840s.

third had successfully terminated; one third were still in operation in 1825; and one third had collapsed with loss to all concerned. In the years leading up to the 1836 Act the methods of the societies evolved considerably in the direction of the prevention of default and the expedition of share distribution.

The three chief methods employed were transferability of shares and obligations; subletting of completed houses; and the borrowing of money by societies from other sources. The first of these grew out of the serious problem created by members whose circumstances changed for the worse during the relatively long period of their obligation to the society. Penal clauses were clearly unenforceable against delinquents without means, so rules were progressively liberalised to permit the sale or transfer of shares. By this means any member in difficulties could leave without serious loss to the society by selling (in effect) his membership to someone else provided the transaction was approved. The second innovation, the letting of completed houses, grew in popularity as the problem of delay in making advances became more irksome.[1] Rents from completed houses were paid into society funds where they swelled the total available for further advances and thus brought the termination of the society nearer: at which time the tenants were evicted and the houses reoccupied by their new owners. The third method simply involved borrowing money from any available source at agreed terms of interest against notes issued by the society. Some indication of the extent to which this method was employed can be gained from the records of the Longridge Society founded in 1793: in its first year of operation subscriptions yielded £155 and borrowing £255. A fourth and much abused method was employed by some societies which involved the substitution of auctions for the more usual ballot in the distribution of shares. Under this system the members made competitive bids for early share issues, sometimes paying a discount (in the form of an advance lower than the face value of the share) of as much as 60%.

For obvious reasons the the number of members in any termin-

---

[1]Cleary (*op cit*) explains this as follows: "If twenty people subscribe ten shillings a month it will be almost ten months before an advance of £100 can be made, and even with the interest on the first advance swelling the funds, it will be nearly as long again before a second £100 can be advanced." The delay in prospect for the twentieth person was not inviting.

ating society tended to be self-limiting. Unless large subscriptions were paid, or small advances taken, or a great deal of additional money obtained, each new member simply prolonged the life of the society. Furthermore the enrolment of new members in later years could only take place if the newcomer agreed to pay an equivalent sum to the subscriptions already paid by existing members since the foundation of the society: an amount either beyond his means or, if within them, one which could probably be better employed in other ways. This limitation, more than any other reason, explains the proliferation of small societies prior to the introduction of permanent societies in 1845. For equally obvious reasons the increase in share trading led to comparisons with joint stock companies, and it was the consequent threat of a stamp duty on share transfers which triggered the 1836 Act.

The interest taken by parliament in the activities of the societies proved to be ultimately beneficial, but it is a reflection on the obscurity of the movement at the time that building society representations to the Chancellor of the Exchequer on the subject of stamp duty proved to be the first indications that gentleman had ever received that such organisations existed. When their purpose had been explained to him, the Chancellor hit upon the expedient of encouraging investment in building societies so as to reduce the funds entering the savings banks which, under government guarantee since 1817, had proved an expensive innovation.[1]

In the years between the passage of the 1836 Act and the Royal Commission of Inquiry into the building societies of 1871, successive governments observed a policy of benign neglect as far as the movement was concerned; although the Friendly Societies formed the subject of legislation on six occasions during the same period. The general view of the authorities appeared to be that their activities were entirely beneficial.

Nonetheless considerable changes took place during the thirty-

[1]The relationship between the building societies and other, government-guaranteed, forms of savings bank has been important ever since; particularly with regard to the setting of interest rates after these became variable during the Great War. The Friendly Societies Act of 1834 permitted the building societies to invest in savings banks, and with the creation of the National Savings Bank the practice developed into a useful safety valve for surplus funds.

five years; the most important being the birth and unprecedented growth of permanent, as opposed to terminating, societies. Because the average life of a terminating society was between ten and fifteen years, the vast majority of the 3500 societies formed between 1836 and 1869 were still of this type; but after 1845 the permanent societies—many of which are still in existence today—began to gain the upper hand. The originator of the permanent idea was an actuary named James Henry James, although it was best expounded and popularised by the founder of the London and Metropolitan Counties Society, Arthur Scratchley. Both these men advocated a rationalisation of one of the last developments of the terminating system, whose disadvantages have been mentioned, which was the automatic creation of a new society (in which late benefitting members of the old could be enrolled as founders, with the expectation of early share allocations) as soon as the back subscriptions required of new members in the old society became an obstacle to membership. Working according to this serial principle the Gould Square Provident Society formed six successive terminating societies between 1844 and 1847. The next step was to convert the original society into a revolving door, so that while individuals could determine the length of their membership on the basis of the sum they wished to borrow, the society itself remained in existence indefinitely—or at least for as long as it was able to attract funds to finance house building or, as was now more often the case, house purchase. Predictably, leading members of the movement challenged the legality of the permanent principle, declaring that the wording of the 1836 Act implied termination; but the registrar of friendly societies approved the rules of James' own Metropolitan Equitable Investment Association in 1845 and a number of permanent societies were formed in its wake.

Despite the clear advantages offered by the permanent societies, and the prospect they offered of a much larger membership than any terminating society, the conservatism of the movement at that time would certainly have restrained and perhaps prevented their growth had it not been for the sudden eruption of another purpose for which the permanent societies were admirably suited: the enlargement of the franchise.

The freehold franchise of the early 19th century was itself a relic of Feudal revisionism, dating from an Act of 1430 whereby

Henry VI had succeeded in removing the power to vote in the County Court from landowners whose holdings were valued at less than forty shillings. This sum, notwithstanding a considerable increase in its real value (it was estimated in 1832 to be worth about £20), remained unchanged for four hundred years until the Great Reform Bill widened the franchise by including certain classes of leaseholder. At the time of the creation of the first permanent building societies demand for further electoral reform had, coincidentally, led to the development of organisations called Freehold Land Societies operating according to friendly society principles, but with the object of financing the purchase of forty shilling plots so as to create voters. Although the origins of the Freehold Land Society movement are believed to extend back to the 17th century,[1] their rise to prominence in the 1840s took place in a spirit of political radicalism unknown in the building society movement, as this extract from a prospectus shows.

"The Grand Objects of this Society are to Improve the Social, Promote the Moral, and Exalt the Political Condition of the Un-enfranchised Millions. It is a lamentable fact that the humbler classes, the industrious millions, know little or nothing of the practical power of the term 'FREEHOLD' and its political relationship to the suffrage! The idea that a Mechanic or labourer could possess a 'Freehold' scarce entered their mind. This society, however, submits a plan for obtaining 'Land for the People,' thus conferring on working men the power of possessing 'FREEHOLD QUALIFICATIONS AS COUNTY VOTERS.' "

The problem with the freehold land societies of the 1840s was that their activities were inhibited by an Act of 1696 which specifically disallowed property purchases intended to create

---

[1] In view of these political overtones it is instructive that the earliest documentary record of the existence of a Freehold Land Society takes the form of an official complaint about the operations of one group called the Norfolk Land Buyers' Society. These persons, whose activities took place about the year 1630, are accused in the complaint of contributing to the destruction of the gentry; the severing of lands from mansions; the raising of prices and rents; the "making of a parity between gentlemen and yeomen," and the "general begetting of pride and stubbornness." See Seymour J. Price *Building Societies* London 1958.

votes. In the view of the courts this meant that if the vendor was aware of the purpose of the purchase, the transaction itself was either invalid or the purchasers themselves were refused a position on the electoral register. That the land societies continued in existence testified to the skill with which they evaded the provisions of the 1696 Act, but it was soon discovered that the methodology of permanent societies provided a perfect cover for the financing of enfranchising property purchases.

The Liberal party was the first to vigorously support land societies and both John Bright and Richard Cobden (who described them as "an engine for extending the franchise") became land society directors. Later the Conservatives entered the field as well, and the consequence of such powerful political influences was a massive increase not only in land societies, but in the business of building societies cooperating with them. This influx of energy and purpose peaked in the mid-1850s and began to decline after the passage of the 1856 Company Act which offered a simpler means of financing: thereafter land societies either died out or turned to the provision of plots for building. Their original purpose disappeared altogether when the household franchise came into effect in 1884.

Freehold land societies and building societies made strange bedfellows although some of them operated in both capacities simultaneously (as indeed did the society with "Grand Objects" cited above), but their political purposes were ultimately incompatible. It is for instance difficult to reconcile the radical tone of "Land for the People" with the following, more sober assessment of the aims of the building society movement intoned by Samuel Smiles in 1864.

"The accumulation of property has the effect which it has always had upon thrifty men; it makes them steady, sober and diligent. It weans them from revolutionary notions, and makes them conservative. When workmen by their industry and frugality, have secured their own independence, they will cease to regard the sight of others' well-being as a wrong inflicted on themselves; and it will no longer be possible to make political capital out of their imaginary woes."

The association of the freehold land societies with the building societies, and the relationship of the former to powerful political figures and men of substance, greatly enhanced the importance of the movement. By 1870 there were over two thousand building societies in existence with 820,000 shareholders and borrowers, and total assets of nearly £20 million.[1] The majority were still terminating societies, but others (including the largest) were permanent, and representatives of both types had begun to embark on more ambitious programmes. The practice of building houses had almost entirely ceased, and with it the influence of the societies on housing types, standards and building methods.[2] Instead they loaned money for the purchase of existing houses; offered construction loans to builders and, more dangerously as it turned out, loaned against the security of commercial and industrial properties.

Expansion itself became the cause of increased government interest; first in the form of efforts to reintroduce stamp duty on mortgage deeds (the duty on share transfers had been staved off in 1836); and later over the very legality of borrowing by societies. As early as 1855 a bill amending and consolidating the Friendly Society Acts appeared with a clause requiring the abolition of all stamp duty exemptions because "It was at first represented that (building) societies were of great use to the poor, but they are now converted into larger speculations for builders and capitalists." After desperate lobbying the clause was withdrawn but the threat remained. Five years later evidence emerged of continuing

---

[1] Comparisons are difficult but according to *The British Economy in Figures 1972* (Lloyds Bank) one pound in 1871 equalled only 14½p one hundred years later. Thus building society assets in 1870 would have a present day value of about £140,000,000. Correspondingly todays building society assets of about £30,000 million would only have been worth £4,350 million in 1870. Even with this correction it can be seen that expansion has been enormous.

[2] The problem of building identical houses for members paying identical sums proved very difficult for the early societies. In many cases their rules were very specific on this point and floor areas, materials etc. were closely controlled. Once members had begun to borrow money to buy the problem disappeared. After 1874 it became illegal for societies to own property other than their offices, and since then the control exercised by them over the design and construction of housing has been relegated to ensuring that the fabric of the dwelling will last for the term of the loan: a duty they have not interpreted innovatively.

government hostility when the Secretary of State solemnly assured another building society deputation that persons deliberately borrowed sums from building societies in order to evade stamp duty.

The storm broke after a Royal Commission appointed to examine the workings of the friendly societies and the building societies made a report in 1872 which drew attention to the important changes that had taken place in society practices since 1836. No longer was there one class of members, all expectant borrowers, but two, borrowers and investors, with the latter greatly outnumbering the former and monopolising the profits generated by the societies' transactions.

To the Liberal government the results of the Royal Commission appeared to show that the differences between the major building societies and joint stock companies had sunk to a matter of unjustified privileges and exemptions in favour of the former. In consequence they put forward a bill in 1873 designed to force the societies either to accept the complete control of the Registrar of Friendly Societies; or else to register under the Companies Act of 1862. At this the movement abruptly lost interest in stamp duty and other imagined grievances and many societies belatedly took the view that the 1836 Act was entirely satisfactory, no further legislation being required. But this government was the famous Liberal administration of 1868–74 which under Gladstone had already pushed through Forster's Education Act, the reform of the universities and the civil service, the partial recognition of the Trades Unions and the legal protection of their funds: its Home Secretary, H. A. Bruce had formed a very clear impression of the nature of the building society movement and was not disposed to retreat.

His intransigence was met by that of the Building Societies Protection Association, an organisation formed in 1870 by the new class of professional managers created by the permanent societies who were not part-time officials and had everything to lose by such a drastic change. Asserting that passage of Bruce's Act in its present form would immediately lead to the collapse of many societies, the Association went on to suggest darkly that the government's real intention was to take over the whole movement and gain control of the many millions of pounds in savings invested with it. This threat, if such it was, unexpectedly evaporated with the general election of 1874 which produced a Conservative government. The change did not avert the threatened legislation but, when it came, the Conservative 1874 Building Societies Act bore no relation to its Liberal counterpart. In return for a concession in the matter of stamp duties the societies lobbied through an Act of their own devising which *The Building Societies' Gazette* joyously described as the movement's "Magna Carta." While all societies were to be placed under the control of the Chief Registrar of Friendly Societies, those already in existence could choose either to incorporate under the Act, or to remain under the provisions of the 1836 Act (many societies did not incorporate, and eight of these were still in existence after World War Two). Societies which did incorporate became legal entities with limited liability, able to *hold* mortgage deeds themselves instead of through trustees acting in their name, but not permitted to *own* property apart from the offices required for the conduct of their business. Borrowing from all sources was limited to two-thirds of mortgage assets (although no penalties were specified for breaches of this rule); and all societies were required to make annual audits and statements of funds to members, and to the Chief Registrar. The penalty for failing to do this, or for making false reports of financial circumstances, was to be a £5 fine.

The movement congratulated the new managerial class: no one foresaw the disasters which were to follow.

3 The Fall of the Liberator

"When the historian comes to deal with this period and to pass judgement upon the influences which have brought about so wonderful a result, he will not overlook the immense work effected by the building society movement in fostering these habits of thrift, of prudence, and of self-control which go to the making of good citizens."

Jubilee Report of the Building
Societies' Association May 1897

Although housing demand was unquestionably the mainspring of the building society movement from its very earliest years, the question of whether houses built by (or with the aid of) societies should be owned or rented was hardly an issue until after the Great War. Even in the years before 1836, when societies themselves owned real estate, the houses were often rented for a time, then taken over by owner-occupiers; or else built with the express purpose of rental by owners who in effect became landlords.

Similarly the connection of the movement with the political fight to extend the franchise made no real distinction between the two forms of tenure. Between 1832 and 1867 it may well have been easier to build a house and own it—thereby becoming a forty shilling freeholder—than to become a voter by paying a rent of more than £50 a year; but thereafter franchise reform was rapid and the distinction between the two ceased to be of political significance.

For these reasons the growth of the building societies in the 19th century was not accompanied by an equivalent growth in owner occupation, even though few other routes to home ownership existed. After 1874 the movement expanded enormously, but the role of home ownership in its expansion was a shadowy one. The building societies have always depicted themselves as institutions straining every nerve to help the common man advance himself by gaining possession of a permanent asset in the form of a home: it is a pose employed today with as great success as at any time in the last two hundred years, yet seldom has it been further from the truth than it was in the last quarter of the 19th century.

The building societies in the 1880s were already financial institutions rather than instruments of thrift, for the innovation of borrowing had changed their character irreversibly: a fact noted by the Royal Commission of 1871 but disregarded in the movement's mythology. In the larger, permanent societies the business of the managers was to attract money from a variety of sources in order to lend it out again against the security of property: borrowing short and lending long, in the terminology of a later time; a process of inherent instability which nonetheless generated the enormous dynamism that the movement enjoyed.[1] Property values were the key to this mechanism, not the virtues of home ownership; and as later generations of speculators were to rediscover, it was sometimes a simple increase in property values which made the difference between a reputation for financial wizardry and a long jail sentence.

Apart from the large national societies responsible for the scandalous crashes to which we shall shortly turn, there were at that time a greater number of small societies which were equally

---

[1] The operations of building societies are dogged by two major problems, both of which periodically create crises for the movement and will continue to do so. With the earliest societies operating on the terminating principle, the greatest disincentive to growth was the slow rate at which subscription funds accumulated and the consequent infrequency of share ballots or mortgage advances. This could simply be characterised as a shortage of funds. Later on in the societies' life, after most members had been loaned money for houses, a second problem arose in the form of finding ways to dispose of the increasing amounts of money coming in to the society through subscriptions, repayments and interest. With the development of permanent societies and the increase in society borrowing, these two problems intensified so that building society management became a matter of ensuring that deposits and borrowings were adequate to cover demand for mortgages and losses through withdrawals, whilst at the same time finding means of "storing" or investing the sums on deposit which tended to accumulate with fluctuations in the housing market. Since 1916 this balance between deposits and loans has been controlled by varying interest rates, but the framework within which these can be changed tends to be narrow.

unsound, though in a rather different way. Part of the irony of the movement's history stems from the fact that although their membership came from that section of the population most directly and passionately concerned with home ownership, the activities of the societies themselves often became synonymous in the Victorian mind with the exercise of chicanery and fraud. The Starr-Bowkett societies provide a good example of this.

Bowkett himself was a doctor in practice in London in 1830. Sincerely concerned with the alleviation of poverty, and passionately committed to the idea of self-help through cooperation, he invented a type of terminating society which generated interest-free loans without borrowing, and which terminated in a little over forty years. Cleary describes his method as follows.

"Let one hundred people form a society with a subscription of 9½d per week: at the end of a year the society will have £205 16s 8d. The members draw lots for an advance of £200 interest free to be secured by a mortgage on house property and the winner, in addition to his subscription, repays about 8s weekly on his advance, clearing the loan in ten years. Weekly subscriptions, plus repayments on the first advance, enable a second draw to take place after a further eleven months. The third, with repayments on two advances flowing in, after a further nine to ten months and so on, until at the end of thirty-one years all members will have had an advance, and after a further ten years the last advance will have been repaid. The total of subscriptions plus any surplus from fines and defaults, less expenses, would then be repaid to the members."

However sound this plan may appear it should be remembered that the poorest workmen—who were to be Bowkett's members—lived in conditions of considerable economic uncertainty from week to week. It required superhuman dedication for them to maintain contributions to a society over such a protracted period and Bowkett was well aware of this. Consequently his societies maintained a savage system of fines and disqualifications for non-payment, in addition to a drastic reduction in running expenses. Scratchley (of permanent society fame) had claimed that management expenses for a society of such size should be about £400 a year: Bowkett ridiculed this figure and insisted on a return to earlier, voluntary principles. Dealt with scathingly by the building society establishment (largely because of his attacks on it), and determined to maintain his spartan regulations, Bowkett made very slow progress in disseminating his ideas: it was not until less scrupulous figures undertook the task of promoting them that they really took off.

The best known promoter was Richard Benjamin Starr, an unsuccessful entrepreneur in many fields before he found his true vocation. Between 1862 and 1891 he founded one thousand Starr-Bowkett societies in England alone, and the idea of them was copied in many other countries. Starr modified Bowkett's system somewhat, and copyrighted his modifications; he made his income from lecture fees, charges for advice, backhanders from solicitors and surveyors, the sale of rule books (printed by his own press) and the compulsory insurance of all society properties with his own insurance company. Just before his death in 1892 he formed a company for the floating of building societies at the rate of 80 a year, which was to yield an annual income of over £3,000.

As can be seen from this description, the rate of failure of these societies was immaterial to the promoter: as indeed was the outcome in terms of home ownership. Starr's seventy-seventh society failed within six weeks of formation and a lecture given by E. W. Brabrook, the assistant Registrar of Friendly Societies, in 1887 suggested that the returns submitted by one Starr society indicated that it was operating as little more than a Bingo club.[1]

"A Star-Bowkett society has completed its third year. Its object, according to the Act, is to make advances to members. It has however not made a single advance. It has received £500 from its members, has declared two appropriations by ballot, paid £130 for them, has spent £120 (on expenses) and has £250 left."

Although the most notorious, Starr was by no means the only well-known building society promoter; his appearances in court— either enforcing his copyright or bringing slander actions— instead of alerting the public merely spread his fame further afield until imitators sprang up in some numbers. Arthur Connor,

[1]Quoted by Cleary (op cit) page 107. Brabrook with Arthur Scratchley (the populariser of permanent societies) co-authored *The Law of Benefit Building Societies* London 1882.

a Yorkshire "philanthropist" floated 260 "Model" societies (for a fee of 65 guineas in each case); Edward Drew launched 53 "Self Help" societies before he was bankrupted in 1889; Edwin Richmond started 89 "Richmond" societies; William Horsley promoted 137 "Perfect Thrift" societies, and a Manchester firm of accountants founded 50 "Popular" societies. Between them "Easy Payment", "Hearth and Home", "Economic" and "Mutual" floated a further three hundred. Unlike Dr Bowkett's original organisations, all the promoter societies stressed the easiness of their terms in the event of illness, unemployment or arrears; a circumstance which contributed to the frequency of failures as well as to the vast number of launches.

There is no period in building society history so distinguished by failures and abuses as the years between 1874 and 1894. So severe was the effect upon public confidence that by the latter date the entire movement was coming apart at the seams and only government intervention saved it.[1] To be sure these disasters took place against a background of unusual uncertainty, for the period was marked by a recession of slowly increasing severity with the general trend of building prices falling from a peak in 1873 to a trough in 1896. With manufacturing depressed there was little demand for industrial capital and a great deal of money found its way into the building societies where it was imagined to be secure against the rock of property value, but this too was crumbling, particularly in the commercial and industrial sectors where (contrary to popular mythology) the larger and more adventurous societies were placing their loans. So widely distributed were the building societies, and so limited were popular means of communication at the time, that the failure of many small societies did not generate any organised demand for reform. Nearly one third of the promoter societies registered after 1874 had dissolved by the end of 1891, as had nearly half of the permanent societies registered during the same period; but it required the collapse of "The Liberator," the greatest crash in building society history, to bring about desperately needed changes.

[1] The figures for the astonishing number of building society failures in the 20 years between the 1874 Act and the remedial 1894 Act given at the foot of this paragraph are taken from Cleary (*op cit*) page 113. The actual numbers are: promoter societies 1581 registered, 423 dissolved; permanent societies 570 registered, 218 dissolved.

"The Liberator Permanent Building and Investment Society," motto *Libera sedes liberum facit* (A free home makes a free man) was founded in June 1868 and later incorporated under the 1874 Act. From the outset its growth was phenomenal; within ten years its gross assets stood at £1 million (about £8 million at present day values), five years later it was the largest society in Britain, more than twice the size of its nearest rival. At the time of its failure in September 1892 "The Liberator" claimed three and a half million pounds worth of mortgage assets alone, equivalent to perhaps £30 million at the time of writing. Its collapse is estimated to have cost the entire building society movement (more than 2700 societies) 20% of their total assets and an incalculable figure in retarded growth stemming from the loss of public confidence. The crash unleashed a flood of attacks on the societies and innumerable homilies on thrift and prudence from the managers of those left unscathed. Notwithstanding the considerable number of failures and abuses which had preceded it, the fall of "The Liberator" alone generated the outrage necessary for parliamentary revision of the "Magna Carta" of twenty years before.

Jabez Spencer Balfour, the founder and managing director of "The Liberator" was a Congregational lay preacher and the son of the founder of one of the first permanent societies. In addition to a reputation as a skilled administrator and publicist, he possessed that capacity for keeping many separate matters in his mind at the same time which makes as often for triumph as for tragedy in the world of finance—especially when wedded to simple philanthropic aims, in his case "that it should be possible for every working man in England to live in his own house, freed from the tyranny of landlordism." Balfour's professional and popular support stayed with him to the end: he was thrice elected to parliament, the last time (in the year of his ruin) by an enormous majority, and he was widely believed to be in line for the position of Postmaster General[1] when the Unionists lost power in 1892.

---

[1] With the exception of Jabez Balfour's clerical connections there are strong similarities between his career and that of John Stonehouse, the former Postmaster General who faked his own drowning when his business machinations threatened to come to light in the autumn of 1974. Both fled to foreign countries and were extradited back to England to stand trial.

He deployed his connections adroitly in the management of "The Liberator": a Viscount was president; four M.Ps were vice-presidents; six ministers and lay preachers were arbitrators, and all the directors held office in one church or another. Furthermore the societies' 500 agencies (Balfour was well ahead of most of his competition in this innovation) were run by clergymen working on commission: during the organisation's 24-year life these gentlemen received £140,000 in commission for the introduction of shareholders and depositors. Balfour also advertised to a degree not seen again among building societies until after the Great War; display notices in the press were continuous, leaflets were distributed wholesale, and an illustrated almanac was issued once a year.

The results were impressive; by 1875 total assets had reached £500,000—a rate of increase without precedent in the history of the movement—but Balfour seems genuinely to have been disappointed in the block to the growth of home ownership which resulted from the prevention of societies *themselves* building by the 1874 Act. He conceived the idea of a total development system in which an independent company would acquire sites and build houses in large numbers, while the financing of the construction of these houses and their subsequent sale on mortgage would generate endless business for "The Liberator." The profits to the company from these sales would provide, in their turn, dividends and directors' fees. Such a company already existed, having been founded before "The Liberator" itself was launched: Balfour took command as managing director and an increasing proportion of "The Liberator's" deposits began to be funnelled into The Lands Allotment Company and another concern, the House and Lands Investment Trust.

By 1881 the number of conventional building society accounts was about 900, but by then the society was already engaged in the financing of huge building projects of the most speculative kind. In 1885, when the total mortgage assets of the society were recorded as over £2 million, the amount outstanding on normal mortgage advances was only £300,000 owed by 623 members. In 1892, the year of disaster, there were barely 200 such accounts owing less than £65,000 although the last published balance sheet claimed mortgage assets of over three million pounds! The vast repercussions of the collapse resulted from the fact that 25,000 depositors and shareholders suffered: mortgage holders were almost non existent.

In the excitement of supporting this crazy structure Balfour lost his original philanthropic drive. His companies built luxury flats and hotels, including the Victoria and the Cecil in London: they commenced the reclamation of 800 acres of land on the Isle of Wight and when the sea wall they built was washed away they added the cost of replacing it to the value of the project. By 1892 Balfour was chairman, director or chief officer of 20 companies and "The Liberator" was entwined with seven of them: one company would obtain an option on some building land, another would buy it at an inflated price, "The Liberator" would pay the bill and Balfour would pocket the profits. Land and buildings were sold from company to company to inflate valuations and when "The Liberator" could not produce enough capital, money was borrowed at ruinous rates of interest from moneylenders— thus relegating the society to the status of second or third mortgagee. If a company could not pay interest due to the society, then the society simply added the sum to the company's loan account, thereby increasing its apparent capital still more. One company, J. W. Hobbs & Co. Ltd., avoided paying £100,000 interest in this way.

Pleased with the progress of the society, depositors and share-holders paid in over £600,000 during 1891—15% more than in the previous year—and the annual report for that year submitted to the Chief Registrar's office spoke of "sound, safe, and substantial progress." But financial collapse had already begun with the failure of Baring's merchant bank (through the default of the Argentine government) in 1890. Although the Treasury and the Bank of England intervened, withdrawals from all savings institutions grew steadily and at the end of 1891 attention was directed to the building societies by the failure of the Portsea Island Society, whose secretary admitted having falsified accounts for nine years. At this withdrawals began in earnest and between January and June 1892 "The Liberator" paid out half a million pounds. On September 2nd a Balfour company, London & General Bank, suspended business and on the same day a letter was sent to all the societies' shareholders and depositors offering to pay withdrawals in rotation: a compulsory winding up order was issued on October 4th. By then Balfour had fled to Genoa.

By Monday September 4th the panic was on. In the course of frenzied withdrawals The London Provident Society and a number of smaller societies folded and by Saturday 10th enormous queues had formed at the doors of The Birkbeck Society, which had developed a banking department of such importance that over £5 million was on deposit while less than half a million was due on mortgage loans. On Monday 12th the Birkbeck was obliged to remain open for thirteen hours disbursing £½ million; business remained heavy until the Wednesday, by which time confidence slowly began to return.[1] But the wound was deep; within a year of "The Liberator" catastrophe membership of incorporated societies had fallen by nearly 10% and the movement as a whole had lost £10 million. A relief fund, with annual appeals, remained in existence until 1922.

A demand for stiff legislation sprang up from all sides: when the directors of "The Liberator" were tried (Balfour was finally extradited from Argentina), none of their offences were concerned with the building society but all with the associated companies. Everything done with "The Liberator" had been perfectly legal under the 1874 "Magna Carta."

A Select Committee was appointed to study four alternative bills (two by private members, one by the government and the last by the Building Societies Association); it reported with an amended version of the government bill which was by far the most strict, calling among other things for public regulation of society business, balloting for advances and second mortgages to be prohibited, dissolution of societies to be within the power of the Chief Registrar and more detailed professional audits. Vigorous lobbying by the Association produced a battery of amendments and the bill was withdrawn in September 1893, but this time the Liberal government did not oblige by dissolving parliament. In 1894 both the Association's bill and the revised government bill were introduced again and referred to a standing committee

---

[1] It is almost certain that without the loan of £½ million in cash from the Bank of England in time for the 13-hour run of 12th September 1892, the Birkbeck Society, with assets of about half the sum claimed by "The Liberator", would have collapsed through simple inability to convert its assets into cash in time. The consequence of two enormous failures within one week would almost certainly have been the destruction of the building society movement.

which found in favour of the latter. On August 25th 1894 the government bill became law.

The sections of the 1894 Act most objected to by the societies were those requiring publication of the extent of mortgage assets on which payments were in arrears (or where properties had already been repossessed) and the deduction of these figures from the total assets used to determine borrowing power. The government's view was that this sort of information was essential if the public were to be able to assess the stability of a society from its published figures. As for the suggestion that speedy foreclosures would cause greater hardship, the government replied that the threat of publication would ensure more care in making advances, and furthermore that losses through foreclosure sales were better faced as soon as possible.

The 1894 Act established a trend for all future building society legislation by simultaneously strengthening the regulatory powers of the Chief Registrar, and giving increasing publicity to the details of building society finances. It did not however mark the end of Liberal displeasure with the movement, for in 1899 Joseph Chamberlain, then Colonial Secretary, introduced a bill intended to furnish local authorities themselves with the powers necessary to advance mortgages for house purchase. This measure could clearly have confronted the building societies with direct and financially sound competition so their response was vigorous. A deputation from the Association called upon Mr Chamberlain in strength and not for the first time government ignorance of the workings of the societies operated in their favour. By claiming that "the majority" of the societies which had been dissolved since 1874 were terminating societies, and (apparently) by concealing the alarming number of permanent societies which had also failed, the deputation succeeded in allaying some of the Colonial Secretary's suspicions. In the event the Bill passed into law but through lack of local authority support achieved negligible results. The principal achievement of the Liberal Party in response to the disasters of the 1880s was therefore the launching of that week-by-week scrutiny of building society finances which has today become an accepted part of popular journalism.

Apart from the alarm caused by the 1899 Act and the final collapse of the Birkbeck in 1911, the twenty years between the 1894 Act and the outbreak of the Great War was a period of relative stagnation in the history of the movement. Even the end of the Birkbeck was by no means as disastrous as that of "The Liberator" for this society, a bank in all but name, ultimately paid out 16s 9½d in the pound to depositors and shareholders.[1] Not only did the 1894 Act prevent many of the old abuses, but the rule against balloting for advances put a stop to the promoters and the rate of formation of new societies plunged. Between 1883 and 1891 an average of 194 societies were incorporated every year: between 1898 and 1914 only 370 were formed in all. As the old terminating societies wound up the total number of societies fell from 3600 in 1895 to 1500 in 1914. Fluctuations in the total assets of the incorporated societies show the effects of loss of public confidence and reduced promotion: from £52 million in 1890 "The Liberator" crash forced the loss of £10 million; thereafter the figure rose again to £76 million in 1910 only to tumble back to £60 million in the wake of the Birkbeck closure, a slow recovery raised the total to £66 million by the outbreak of war. The number of shareholders and borrowers followed a somewhat similar pattern but the decline set in earlier, from an estimated 820,000 in 1870 the number fell to 650,000 in 1890 and then to 580,000 in 1900; from then until 1914 the number increased slowly to 618,000. It was not until 1928 that separate figures for borrowers were included in returns.

By 1914 the building society movement had been in existence for 140 years. Notwithstanding the speculative activities of many societies and their directors, and the increasing emphasis on depositors rather than borrowers, the ostensible aim of the movement did not change in that time. From the anonymous Birmingham fathers of the first society to the notorious Jabez Balfour, all had pledged allegiance to the extension of home ownership in an

---

[1]Numerous exceptions had been made to the provisions of the 1894 Act in order to permit the Birkbeck"Bank" to continue to operate with a very low (7% at time of failure) mortgage asset compared to deposits: other societies being confined to the two thirds rule. A simple change of the name from building society to bank could have realised the Birkbeck's actual role and spared the building society movement another disaster. Some mystery surrounds the 1911 crash, as the initial run was started by anonymous letters sent to shareholders. These were countered by rumours that the Bank of England was to step in as it had in 1892: unfortunately unfounded.

era when rental was overwhelmingly the dominant form of tenure, and landlordism the villain of popular mythology. What then was the concrete result in terms of home ownership of this century of effort?

Surprisingly even as late as 1914 the distribution of tenure in England and Wales appears to be uncertain. Cleary derives his estimate[1] from an extrapolation of information contained in the Ministry of Health Departmental Committee on Valuation for Rates report of 1939. This committee found when collecting data on houses built before 1914 and still in use, that 1.44 million were owner-occupied. Since the 1911 census recorded 7.75 million dwellings of all types, Cleary takes as his starting point the assumption that all owner-occupied houses built before 1914 were still owner-occupied in 1938 and thus 19% of pre-war dwellings were owner-occupied. This determines his highest possible percentage, but as many of these pre-1914 dwellings became owner-occupied after the Great War he concludes that the real 1914 figure must be significantly lower. After allowing for certain classes of dwelling excluded from the Departmental Committee's survey which were owner-occupied in 1914 (such as flats over shops), and making a further allowance for demolitions in the inter-war period, he finally suggests that between 10–15% is the closest possible estimate. He also cites an *Economist* report which concludes that only 10% of all house building prior to 1914 was for owner occupation.

If as little as 10% of the housing in England and Wales (approximately 775,000 dwellings) was owner-occupied in 1914, it is tempting to try to compute the percentage that *could* have been owner-occupied early in the previous century, for when allowance is made for the enormous population increase which took place between the end of the war with Napoleon and the outbreak of the Great War, it appears more than possible that despite the protestations of the building society movement, not only did no increase in owner-occupation occur, but on the contrary, there was a decrease.

Unfortunately, the only possible means of arriving at an estimate of the percentage of freehold dwellings in existence early in the 19th century is by way of the size of the electorate prior to

[1]Cleary (*op cit*) page 184.

the first major franchise reform of 1832. By subtracting the increase in the number of voters generated by the reform Acts of 1884, 1867 and 1832 from the known electorate of 5 millions created by the 1884 household franchise, it is possible to conclude that in the entire United Kingdom (which at that time included the whole of Ireland) there were 1.3 million freehold electors on the eve of the Great Reform Bill of 1832. Subtracting from this figure those voters in Scotland and Ireland (according to an average of constituencies and population) and making an allowance for the effective doubling of population which occurred between the census of 1831 and the census of 1881, it appears that between 400,000 and 650,000 freehold voters were distributed amongst the 2.9 million households recorded in the 1831 census for England and Wales. This calculation suggests that between 13% and 22% of the households in England and Wales were forty shilling freeholders before the passage of the first building societies Act.

Both the estimate for owner-occupation for 1914 and the estimate for 1831 (the latter of course disputable) are interesting in relation to the major political strategies discussed in chapter one. It is customary to dismiss the public sector contribution to housing output prior to 1914 as insignificant—a bare 14,000 dwellings were built by local authorities between the Housing of of the Working Classes Act of 1890 (the first to permit construction with public funds[1]) and the outbreak of war—but it is less common to concede that the contribution made by the building society movement to home ownership over a much longer period was equally insignificant.

No one doubts that the building societies played a part in multiplying the number of dwellings in England and Wales from 2.48 million in 1831 to 7.75 million in 1911, but it was not until the entire environment in which they operated had been transformed by the greatest war in history that home ownership really began to increase, and their role in the process became crucial.

[1]Berry (*op cit*) points out that under the 1890 Act the entire cost of public sector construction was borne by local rate payers and in order to minimise this burden any houses so built were to be sold into the private sector within 10 years.

Part Two

Fanfare for the Common Man

4 A Dose of Morphine

"What is at the back of this desire for better housing? It is nothing less than our unfortunate British climate, which we want to shut out . . . If a miner came out of the mine near the bay of Naples the circumstances of his life would be totally different . . . because almost any kind of housing would do in a climate which did not drive you indoors . . . I would like to take a deputation of miners to the city of Rome and show them the baths of Caracalla. Why not erect in every mining centre something of the same kind? For £40 million one could cover the country with these things. Why not have, not the holes in which the English people bathe, but magnificent warm pools, as I have seen them in some foreign resorts, with floating chess boards and card tables, where people can disport themselves in nice warm water in comfortable surroundings?"

Sir Martin Conway MP,
Debate on the Housing and Town
Planning Act 1919

The Great War of 1914–18 created the modern state-controlled economy and broke the political power of 19th-century capital; although the irreversibility of both events was not accepted for many years. Because the onset of the war was so sudden, its conduct so unprecedentedly total, and its duration so unforeseen, the policies pursued by British wartime governments were little more than assemblies of desperate measures, dragged under fear of extinction from a parliament which would in normal times have considered none of them. The seizure of private overseas assets, the control of investments and savings, control of currency and exchange rates, control of prices and incomes, effective nationalisation of mines and railways, centralised collective bargaining, graduated taxation, rent control, food rationing and compulsory military service; all were wartime measures enacted in a state of emergency but destined to form the vocabulary of political and economic policy, in peace and war, from that time forth. It made no difference when the armistice finally came that those unable to grasp the magnitude of the changes which had occurred tried repeatedly to turn the clock back by reducing Armageddon to a capital loss to be made good by one means or another. Internationally their efforts to force the Central Powers to pay for the war merely laid the foundations for a second conflict, more disastrous for capital than the first. Domestically they paid for their failure to pay for the war out of current taxation by the inheritance of a crushing burden of debt which in turn led to the Great Depression. Only those who saw the disruption itself as a victory were able to see the futuristic nature of the means employed to fight it.[1]

For them the social changes wrought by public expenditure, high wages, full employment and egalitarian legislation could be set on the credit side of the balance sheet. For the mass of the people there were no "good old days" to be regained at almost any cost: the war had raised both their status and their power, enabling many to earn and save for the first time in their lives. However grave the economic circumstances in the twenty years following the armistice, conditions never again sank to the level prevalent before 1914. The older statistical surveys of Booth and Rowntree

[1] Alan S. Milward (*The Economic Effects of the Two World Wars on Britain* London 1970) summarises what he calls the classical interpretation in a quotation from Hirst and Allen (*British War Budgets* 1928) "The Great War brought a load of debt, taxes and misery incalculable. The expenditure during the four years that it lasted reached a total incomprehensible and inconceivable to the ordinary mind." Inconceivable or not, the econimists of the classical school endeavoured to estimate these costs in the process of calculating the reparations to be paid by the Central Powers, principally Germany. In an actuarial study of unprecedented grandeur E. L. Bogart (*Direct and Indirect Costs of the Great World War* 1920) evaluated the capital loss of 616,000 British servicemen killed and 1,656,000 injured at 4140 dollars per man. Including other estimated costs, and deducting an estimated five years peacetime expenditure, Bogart finally concluded that the war had cost Britain 44 billion dollars: efforts to extract this sum from the losers proved futile. In a characteristic gesture the future Conservative Prime Minister Stanley Baldwin gave £120,000—one-fifth of his personal fortune—towards paying off the National Debt in 1919.

show that it was all too possible for men to be in full employment in Edwardian times yet dying of malnutrition through poverty, while for those intermittently employed or unemployed this condition was normal. Apart from isolated cases these conditions never returned after 1918, and it is a measure of the democratisation that the war had brought about that even in the depths of the Depression this remained true.

It is as a struggle between the popular forces unleashed by the war and the conservative forces endeavouring to return to a status quo which grew increasingly idealised with the passage of time, that the evolution of housing policy and in particular the emergence of home ownership as a mass phenomenon can best be seen.

The conventional wisdom, which is by no means inaccurate, is to regard the passage of the Increase of Rent and Mortgage Interest (War Restrictions) Act in December 1915 as the commencement of substantive government involvement in housing. All previous measures, such as the 19th-century Public Health Acts, or the 1890 Housing of the Working Classes Act, left the free market in housing intact: although the former burdened it with additional costs which were passed on to rent payers, and the latter foreshadowed the provision of housing from public funds. The rent control Act was quite different in two particulars: first because it was to be a temporary measure, expiring six months after the end of the war; and second because it was applied retroactively, holding rents and mortgate interest rates at their level on 3rd August 1914, the day before the outbreak of war. In the event the relief generated by the first of these particulars proved premature (at the time of writing rent control has been in continuous existence for 62 years, although the war ended 60 years ago), while the alarm expressed by landlords at the retrospective clause[1] proved all too well founded (the same 60 years has seen the virtual extinction of the private landlord).

[1] It is an indication of the ambiguity of the building societies with regard to rental at this time that their reaction to a piece of legislation which, more than any other, launched the owner-occupation boom which has continued till the present day, was to describe it as "The gravest act of injustice ever inflicted by the British Parliament." The author of that statement being not merely the Manager of the Temperance Building Society, but also a director of a property company owning 7,000 rented houses. (Cleary (*op cit*) page 173).

The immediate causes of the 1915 Act were serious enough in all conscience. Military mobilisation and a massive increase in the production of war materials of all kinds had led to large population movements reminiscent of the demographic changes of a century before. At the same time house building, already depressed in the years immediately preceding the war, had virtually ceased. Sudden pressure on the housing market in certain cities led to rapid increases in rents and consequent evictions: in Glasgow the issue became so serious that rent strikes and open rioting broke out. Clearly at a time when a citizen army was being mobilised and workers enjoyed more real power than ever before (by virtue of the vital necessity for their labour) civil peace could hardly be enforced by the military: thus a measure swept unchecked through parliament which in peace time would never have achieved the status of a private member's bill.

Yet the blow was not entirely unprecedented: the political power of the landlords had already been destroyed by universal suffrage; now it was the turn of their economy, which was to be starved to death by an unique and universal restraint of trade. For whatever the intentions of the wartime government as to the temporary nature of rent control, it rapidly became evident as the struggle progressed that only an economic miracle could remove it. By the end of 1917 prices had risen 125% above the level of 1914 and a year later (when rent control was supposed to lapse) they stood at 225%. At the end of 1918 with revolution raging in two formerly combatant countries and an embittered conscript army awaiting demobilisation, rent increases of that order were a political impossibility. The government was hooked, for rent control was indeed "like a dose of morphine."[1]

---

[1]The aphorism "rent control is like a dose of morphine" was coined by Edith Elmer Wood (*Recent Trends in American Housing* New York 1931) but it serves to epitomise the traditional view of the importance of rent control. More recent writers tend to minimise its effect on the decline of the private rental sector by citing the shift in investment away from housing and the consequent decline in output before 1914, and the fact that new housing after 1918 was *not* subject to rent control. The problem here is that an important psychological factor is ignored. The drastic wartime controls, including rent control, had thoroughly alarmed the rentier class: if their income from rents had been throttled once, it could be throttled again under any pretext (which of course it was, within twenty years at the beginning of World War Two). Their answer was to

Committed to some involvement in post-war housing, of an as yet unspecified but inevitably substantial kind, the wartime government found other reasons to develop its interest in the domestic environment. Inventories of manpower resources revealed that an alarmingly high proportion of conscripts from depressed urban areas were unfit for military service; 1.6 out of 2.4 million school children medically examined were unfit, and boys from preparatory schools averaged five inches taller than their state school counterparts. Clearly the capacity to fight a total war depended on manpower; soldiers, sailors, workmen and (for the first time) workwomen: equally clearly bad and inadequate housing was not only a cause of unrest but a military and logistical liability. In August 1917 a Ministry of Reconstruction was set up under Dr Christopher Addison, a Liberal politician who was soon to give his name to a housing bill scarcely less drastic than the rent control measures of 1915.

Meanwhile "the gravest act of injustice ever inflicted by the British Parliament" (as their leader described rent control) was causing difficulties to the building societies; but they, with characteristic ingenuity, contrived to turn it to their ultimate advantage. From the very beginning of the war the movement had feared a flight of capital which might occur if government interest rates greatly exceeded their own, which had remained constant for a period scarcely credible in the light of modern experience.[1] In order to avoid this situation various means of effectively increasing interest rates to borrowers were developed, some with and some without government assistance. In the latter case mortgage holders were offered a chance to renegotiate their loans at higher rates (with the unspoken alternative of foreclosure after the war), and in the former the term of the loan was increased so that repayments remained the same. At the time many societies

sell and to build for sale, a response brought about by the shock of the retrospective clause in the 1915 Act. The arguments over the significance of rent control are well summarised by Berry (*op cit*) pages 112–114.

[1] In the year of writing (1977) the mortgage interest rate charged by the societies changed four times in ten months. Whereas Cleary (*op cit*) notes that the Halifax Permanent charged 4½–5 % to borrowers for 56 *years*, from 1859 to 1915. The abandonment of the fixed interest mortgage was one of the most far reaching changes in building society practice brought about by the Great War.

found that they did not possess the power under their own rules to adjust rates upward at all, and this omission was speedily remedied.

These novel methods of control did not however prevent the threatened loss of assets to government securities; what did save the societies was the virtual cessation of construction, which drastically reduced the demand for mortgages at the same time as withdrawals and low investment were depleting reserves. At such a reduced level of business repayments of existing mortgages provided sufficient income to maintain a balance, with the result that the total assets of the movement increased marginally from £66.2 million in 1914 to £68.5 million four years later. In the process the societies themselves accumulated government securities, The Halifax Permanent, at the time the largest society, increased its government holdings from £15,000 in 1914 to £1.3 million in 1918.

By 1917 the societies, like the government, were looking forward to the construction needs of the post-war period. Opinions within the movement differed; some (in the spirit of Jabez Balfour) wanted the socieities to take the lead in planning large housing developments, putting up 80% of the finance themselves and inviting builders to find the remainder. Others felt certain that building costs would be very high in the immediate post-war years, only to fall later taking prices and rents with them; a situation which would discourage investment in building to let unless the government offered a subsidy of some kind. The chairman of the Building Societies Association conference of 1917 offered a word of caution: building houses for the lower paid worker would require "special solutions ... whether or not building societies should mix themselves up in it, required very careful consideration ... They must not prejudice the high position in which they stood among the financial institutions of the country."[1]

Everything now depended on the housing policy of the post-war government; for the demands of the conscript army, the loss of four years' construction and maintenance, and the ravages of rent control all pointed to the need for drastic measures. Speaking in Wolverhampton at the end of the war the Liberal coalition

[1] Cleary (*op cit*) page 178.

premier David Lloyd George asked dramatically "What is our task?" And then answered "To make Britain a fit country for heroes to live in!" The answer was soon rendered into the slogan "Homes for Heroes" with which the Liberal coalition fought and won the December 1918 general election. With a last display of the reforming zeal of earlier Liberal governments they did not disappoint their khaki supporters.

The plan was breathtaking in its simplicity and had little to do with the building societies. Dr Addison, translated from Minister of Reconstruction into Minister of Health, was to assume responsibility for the construction by local authorities of half a million dwellings in three years. The houses were to be paid for out of the proceeds of a penny rate augmented by such assistance from the Treasury as proved necessary, and were to be let at controlled rents. Local authorities themselves were to determine the number of dwellings required in their own administrative areas. For the building societies, pretending concern for their high position as financial institutions, but in fact enraptured by the prospect of advancing money for private investment in houses to let at market rents, this was a severe blow. Dr Addison's programme, which became law with the passage of the Housing and Town Planning Act of August 1919, went far with its limitless government subsidy to increase that very inflation in building costs which was so feared during the war years: worse still the impossibility of removing rent controls was finally officially recognised and the 1915 Act was renewed. Even the direct subsidy to private builders for rental housing, wrung out of the government by the building societies in the Housing (Additional Powers) Act, failed to attract large-scale development because fears of a price collapse were now too strong.

Meanwhile the local authorities, backed by Dr Addison and the limitless resources of the Treasury, were exploring their new found powers. In response to the urgency of the Act they had supplied within two months of its passage housing programmes for more than 1000 council districts. By the summer of 1920 contracts had been agreed for 170,000 houses at figures ranging from an average of £770 per house in July 1919 to £920 one year later. In everything except the cost of the enterprise the Minister of Health was right on target; but the government took alarm at the massive increases in public spending and "Homes for Heroes," like other Liberal programmes, went down before the Geddes axe that autumn. With the removal of the open-ended Treasury subsidy the brief post-war boom came to a sudden end and the Addison Act was cut short at 174,000 houses.[1]

Against this background of public sector birth, boom and bust the first faint signs of life in the owner-occupier market passed almost unnoticed. Even while the building societies were bewailing the lack of private building for rental through the malevolent influence of rent control, that same "temporary" measure was beginning to drive another kind of business their way: business that within a decade was to grow from a barely perceptible trickle to an unprecedented gusher of wealth.

The shape of what was to become a staple of building society business became clear very soon after the first extension of rent control in 1919, although it took time to build up to full volume. Delayed and expensive repairs coupled with controlled rents presented post-war landlords with a poor return on their investment; there was thus a strong incentive for them to sell as soon as their property became vacant, or alternatively to try to sell to the tenants they could not remove. Either way the building societies stood to gain mortgage business. Furthermore, with the appearance of two sets of values for houses—those with and those without vacant possession—there were clearly opportunities for speculation. Rent controlled houses could be bought cheaply and sold expensively, provided the tenants could be induced to depart.

Together these simple practices (whether carried out benignly or with something approaching duress) were to dismantle the apparently impregnable rentier structure of 1914 within fifty years.

Amongst the movement's leaders there was some opposition to this new turn of events, however closely its proponents could make it appear to conform to the earliest aims of the societies in the matter of the virtues of home ownership. *The Building Societies'*

[1]With 170,000 houses contracted in its first year, the Addison Act was conceivably on target for 500,000 dwellings in three years; but between 1st January 1919 and 31st December 1922 only 210,257 houses were completed. The Labour government's post World War Two programme, which called for twice as many houses in the same period of time, did not achieve its target either but did rather better with 780,493 permanent and temporary completions between 1st January 1946 and 31st December 1949.

Gazette for December 1921 carried a bitter protest describing "dealings and speculations in connection with houses" as a "disgrace to our civilization" and exhorting the societies to lend to local authorities instead; but the results of the sale of rental properties were impossible to ignore. Building society advances on mortgage rose rapidly from £7 million in 1918 to £25 million in 1920 and although the slump which followed reduced new business somewhat, rising deposits and high non-mortgage assets (inherited from the war) enabled the more far sighted society managers to contemplate a rent-controlled future with confidence.

Not that many then expected rent control to continue for as long as it did. With the disintegration of the Liberal coalition and the election of a Conservative government in 1922 politics took an abrupt turn to the right, with talk of the dismantling of war-time controls, further cuts in government spending and an end to the "pampering of labour" so as to restore capitalism to its pre-war vigour. Amongst the measures proposed was the pro-gressive removal of rent controls; an idea so unpopular with the electorate that the Conservative Minister of Health (responsible for housing) lost his seat at a by-election as a result. The removal of rent control was immediately postponed and a new Minister (Neville Chamberlain) was directed to attack the housing shortage without further ado. The ensuing Housing Act of 1923 was a humiliating admission by the champions of private enterprise that the much-criticised state involvement in housing begun by their predecessors was unavoidable, at least for the present.

The Chamberlain Act, which with some modification was eventually to lead to the construction of 420,000 dwellings, was an ingenious measure offering a 20-year subsidy to local authorities and private builders with no contribution from the rates: but local authority construction was only to be approved if the Minister could be convinced that private enterprise could not do the job. As a result virtually all the early Chamberlain Act houses were built for sale, to which end the local authorities were empowered to guarantee building society loans to private builders. Not surprisingly few of these houses found their way into the hands of those whose predicament lay at the root of the problem, and in consequence rent control continued, with each passing year adding to the numbers of those landlords who had ceased to believe in the return of the good old days.

With the coming of the first Labour government in 1924 the idea implicit in both the Addison and Chamberlain Acts, that one short but powerful state-aided housing effort would suffice to undo the effects of the war and restore a free housing market, was abandoned for the first time. Unlike Dr Addison (who had provided for the construction of 500,000 houses in 3 years) and Neville Chamberlain (whose subsidy had also only been made available for three years); John Wheatley, the Labour Minister of Health, introduced the Housing (Financial Provisions) Act of 1924, which not only proposed a subsidy period of 15 years, but also removed the private enterprise stipulations of the Chamberlain Act and extended its subsidy period to match. At the same time Wheatley concluded a long term "gentleman's agreement" with the building unions intended to increase the supply of skilled workmen.

Designed to subsidise the local authority construction of dwellings for public rental at controlled rents, the Wheatley Act, which eventually led to the construction of 520,000 houses, reintroduced the combined rate and Treasury subsidy of the Addison Act but avoided any open-ended commitment by limiting both to a fixed figure to be paid as a lump sum; the Treasury component to be repaid over 40 years. This attempt to establish a long-term housing programme was not however destined to last its 15 years. The Labour government was short-lived and Conservative economics reasserted itself as the Great Depression approached. In 1927 both Chamberlain and Wheatley subsidies were reduced and two years later the Chamberlain Act was repealed. The Wheatley Act, protected briefly by the Labour government of 1929, went the same way in 1933. With them passed the first attempt to enable poor people to live in expensive houses by means of publicly subsidised construction carried out by the local authorities. The idea was not to be revived until 1946.

The winding down of the great government housing programmes (and the confession of their failure implicit in the continuation of rent control) made apparent the true extent of the switch from rental to ownership which was now taking place. While the economists and politicians of the old school consoled themselves with lingering hopes that reduced demand through falling population would at last restore the stability of 1914, an increasing rate of household formation continually falsified their wishes. Despite unemployment which averaged 12% between 1921 and 1930 and rose to 20% in 1931, housing demand did not fall and building for private rental did not become profitable; moreover combined housing output (public and private sectors) fell rapidly from a peak of 270,000 units in England and Wales in 1927 to a trough of 160,000 in 1930. And yet the building societies prospered. The total assets of the movement rose from £68 million in 1919 to nearly £300 million 10 years later, and over the same period annual mortgage advances rose by 200% to a figure greater than the assets of all building societies in 1914.

And this was only the beginning. Apart from the continuing effect of rent control, which has been discussed, there were other powerful factors at work which conspired to make the 1930s a decade of unprecedented expansion both for the societies and for home ownership; although as before the interest taken by the former in the latter was not all that it seemed.

One direct consequence of rent control was of course a dire shortage of new housing built to let, so even new households with incomes adequate to pay market rents frequently found it easier to buy than to take the traditional route. Correspondingly money which a generation before might have been invested in building houses to rent, found its way instead into building society shares. With the increasing profundity of the Depression alternative forms of investment ceased to be competitive and the influx into the building societies between 1931 and 1936 (when the yield on government securities began to rise again) exceeded all previous records. From 1928 to 1938 the number of depositors increased 2.3 times and the number of shareholders almost doubled: shareholding indeed had to be controlled by a system of rationing in the worst years of the Depression.

This rapid increase in available funds, which reached a peak with total assets for the movement as a whole standing at £773 million on the outbreak of World War Two, clearly created an embarrassment of wealth for the societies. Depression conditions not only fuelled deposits but drastically reduced the number of possible mortgagors: commerce and industry were on their knees, local authority borrowing had barely begun before the relevant Acts were repealed, and the landlords were selling up instead of borrowing to finance new construction. By the late 1920s these combined pressures had created a situation in which the only release for society funds was the business generated by transfers from rented stock to owner-occupation, and this was hardly adequate. The process of obtaining vacant possession or inducing tenants to buy was slow and hedged with legal restrictions, furthermore the selling landlords were a diminishing asset: in the end it appeared that the only answer for the societies was to promote the building of new houses for sale as fast as possible. Only unprecedented rates of new building could absorb the funds at the societies disposal, and from this need sprang the great speculative housing boom of the 1930s.

The societies began a campaign for the promotion of owner occupation with a zeal not seen since the time of "The Liberator." Advertising, once discreet or non-existent, burst forth in new and outrageous forms. In 1913 the Co-operative Permanent Society had spent £410 on printing, stationery and advertising; for 1931 the figure was £28,000—nearly £20 out of every £1000 of assets— and the figures rose higher still throughout the decade before the war. Branch offices too were expanded enormously. The Halifax trebled the number of its agencies and branches between 1919 and 1939 and when its City of London office opened in 1931 The Lord Mayor with coach, postillions and outriders attended to perform the ceremony. The Abbey Road society drew public attention to its annual meetings by inviting celebrities as guests of honour, and put on lavish and extravagant displays at successive Ideal Homes Exhibitions.[1]

In addition to these high-profile activities the societies endeavoured to extend their lending business by more direct methods. The percentage of the valuation of a house that any society would lend had always varied according to the circumstances of the borrower, the condition and location of the property and other considerations. Advances beyond 80% of the valuation were rare and the remaining 20%, plus solicitor's fees and other closing costs, was often an insuperable obstacle to sales. The societies therefore revived the practice (first employed during the hazardous 1880s) of taking collateral security on the mortgage loan so as to increase the percentage of the valuation that could be advanced. The Chamberlain Act of 1923 had already empowered local

---

[1]These examples are cited by Cleary (*op cit*) page 192.

authorities to make such guarantees, but little use had been made of the opportunity: instead it fell to the insurance companies to develop the measure. In its most popular form insurance company collateral, purchased by a single premium, guaranteed the society against any loss above 70% or 75% of the valuation which might result from default and sale. This simple expedient enabled the society to advance 85% or 90%. Variations of the same principle involved guarantees arranged with employers to cover mortgages to employees; life assurance policies; trustee securities and even preference shares. Another 19th-century practice, the payment of commissions for the introduction of mortgage business, also revived during this frenzied period.

However none of these methods achieved the results or created the difficulties that resulted from the invention of the "builder's pool". This cartel arrangement came about as a result of the difficulties faced by builders after the repeal of the various subsidy Acts in the early 1930s. With the near certainty (at that time) of selling any house they could put up, the builders wanted some way to obtain the full price of the house from the building society. The method proposed involved both risks and advantages for society and builder, for in its simplest form it was merely a collateral payment by the builder to the society so that the buyer could receive a 100% mortgage. Clearly there were risks of default and openings for corruption, but the outstanding practical success of the method silenced all criticism for a time. The society in any case played no part in the arrangements reached between the builder and the buyer, merely receiving a "joint deposit" from the builder equal to the difference between the valuation of the house and the purchase price. This deposit was repaid upon receipt of an agreed number of mortgage payments from the buyer.

In this simple form the "builder's pool" would seem to be of little advantage to the builder, except to enable him to sell houses at a discount. In practice however it was customary for the society only to take the "joint deposit" on the first batch of houses built, thereafter advancing full purchase price on the "personal guarantee" of the now-presumed-to-be-trustworthy builder. In this form the advantage seems to have reversed into the builder's favour; but in practice the society generally contrived to keep a balance of "joint deposits" in its possession sufficient to cover any default. By this ingenious means societies and builders became bound together according to an infinite variety of secret arrangements, with each endeavouring to pressure the other into accepting less advantageous terms.

However murky the waters in which buyers, builders, lenders and investors were now swimming, there could be no doubt that the results in terms of bricks and mortar were impressive. Four million new houses were built between 1919 and 1939, just over one million of them with the aid of government subsidies of one kind or another, but the vast majority of the remainder by private enterprise for sale to owner occupiers. And here success was piled upon success as the end of the era approached. From a Depression nadir of 110,000 completions in 1930, private builders pushed the figure up to 200,000 in 1933 and finally a pre-war record of 270,000 in 1935. Thereafter completions fell off somewhat, but the average for the period 1933–39 was 240,000 houses a year—a record unsurpassed before or since.

If the total interwar achievement, an increase of 50% in the number of dwellings in England and Wales (from 7.75 to 11.4 million), was remarkable, the growth in home ownership which had accompanied it was truly staggering. By 1938, the year in which accurate estimates of tenure distribution first become possible,[1] the combined effects of rent control, falling prices, inconclusive politics and ambitious building society leadership had brought an increase of 384% from the popularly accepted 1914 figure of 775,000 owner-occupied dwellings to a measured 3.75 million. From a minority of perhaps 10% at the outbreak of the Great War, home ownership had grown to account for one third of all housing[2] by 1939. The increase over twenty years of peace

[1] These estimates are based on the returns made by local authorities for the Departmental Committee on Valuation for Rates (the Fitzgerald Committee; *Report to the Minister of Health by the Departmental Committee on Valuation for Rates 1939*, published in 1944).

[2] There appear to be two different assessments of the extent of owner-occupation in England and Wales immediately prior to the Second World War. Cleary (*op cit* 1965) and the DOE *Housing Policy Review* Technical Volume 1 (1977) work from the Fitzgerald Committee report published in 1944. The Housing Research Foundation (*Home Ownership in England and Wales* 1970) and Halsey (*Trends in British Society since 1900* Macmillan 1972) give much lower figures which suggest only 23%. The higher figure seems to me more convincing.

had wiped out the gains made by rental in the preceding one hundred.

The building societies and rent control shared about equally in their responsibility for this revolution. Forty per cent of the new owner-occupiers were current mortgage holders (in 1928 the entire movement had boasted only 500,000 borrowers, 10 years later there were one and a half million); the rest were either the owners of pre-1914 dwellings, or sitting tenants who had purchased with cash or private mortgage from landlords eager to dispose of once valuable investment properties. This last, a vast but diminishing reservoir of potentially saleable dwellings, has remained a source of building society business until the present day, although increasing age and poor maintenance have made it progressively less attractive. For the societies in the late 1920s and throughout the 1930s new building was the prime outlet for their accumulating assets.

In 1928 they loaned £70 million to 164,000 borrowers; in 1933 advances to 250,000 house buyers totalled £103 million; in 1936, a record year, 312,000 buyers borrowed £140 million. To be sure by the end of the decade there was evidence that other forms of investment were again beginning to compete with the societies for funds; there was also evidence that demand created by the collapse of building for private rental was finally being overtaken by the glut of houses on the market (with the paradoxical result that some were rented by builders in desperation); but the resources of the movement were now ten times larger than in 1914 and, as a result of several years of aggressive promotion, home ownership could for the first time be regarded as a popular alternative to private rental.

5 The New Jerusalem

"The whole concept of the AIROH house is based on the suitability for house building of methods of construction and assembly developed in the course of wartime aircraft production ... Some will complain that the result has little in its appearance to recall the taut lines of the Spitfire or of the Beaufighter. It must be conceded that the design has not yet in outward expression fully found itself. That is not the point. What is much more significant is that the minds which have created the modern aircraft have turned their attention to the solution of an equally urgent problem."

John Madge *Tomorrow's Houses* 1946

While it is true that the previously insubstantial cause of home ownership was transformed into a mass phenomenon by the activities of the building societies between the wars, it cannot be said to have attracted any great enthusiasm on the part of popular forces in British politics during the same period. The Labour party, heirs to the Liberal tradition of radical reform, steadfastly adhered to the principles of public rental and private rent control which had emerged from the Great War, and were only converted to an acceptance of ownership as a matter of political necessity in the 1960s. For socialist thinkers, and indeed for many others, ownership was conceived as a middle-class phenomenon and an evasion of the heart of the housing problem, which was clearly a matter of the production of better and more numerous houses to let at rents that poor people could afford. That ownership had grown dramatically was seen as evidence of the failure of public housing policy, particularly during the years of Conservative rule prior to the Churchill coalition of 1940.

Seen from the Left the achievements of the private builders in their alliance with the building societies were contaminated by speculation and exploitation. Those who had bought houses were either in no real need of them or else had been forced into owner-ship by the absence of suitable rented dwellings. The view that the new owner-occupiers were so under duress enjoyed much support in the 1930s—even from within the building society movement[1]—and much was made of the abuses which led to the societies' voluntary code of practice (drawn up in 1936), and the Borders' case which, in combination with the Building Societies Act of 1939, finally put an end to the "builder's pool" and allied practices.

The celebrated case began with an action brought by the Brad-ford Third Equitable Benefit Building Society in the summer of 1937 to possess a house mortgaged to Mrs Elsy Florence Eva Borders, the wife of a London taxi driver, who was three months in arrears on her mortgage payments. As a result of numerous appeals and counter appeals it was finally concluded by a judge-ment of the House of Lords in May 1941. The substance of the successive actions revolved around the legality of the original mortgage which had been made by the society in the proportion of 95% of the purchase price, with the aid of a deposit made by the builders Messrs Morrell (Builders) Ltd. But the mainspring of Mrs Borders' protest against eviction was the poor construction of the house, for which she held the society partly responsible as a result of a brochure issued by the builders to the following effect:

"Morrell (Builders) Ltd are the only builders in Great Britain who can offer by special arrangement with a leading building society, a 95% MORTGAGE advance over a period of 24 years at 5% interest. This proves without a shadow of doubt, the amazing value of Morrell houses."

---

[1]Cleary (op cit) quotes Walter Harvey writing in The Building Societies' Gazette for March 1942. ". . . they (the societies) were drawn off financing the building of houses to let by the much more profitable business of financing house purchase at scarcity prices, mainly for the benefit of the builder–seller. Several types of collateral security were devised to back up the lending of an unduly high proportion of purchase prices . . . The mistake made by the building societies had been that they had a greater regard for the builder-vendor than the buyer-borrower, who in many cases had been induced, by the difficulty of renting a home, to take on mortgage obligations too onerous for his means."

The combination of a female litigant (who conducted her own case in court), a charge of "jerry building" (widely alleged of speculative builders at the time) and the acknowledged legal uncertainties of the "builder's pool", gave the case considerable popular appeal. After much press activity in Mrs Borders' favour a number of other purchasers of defective houses also brought actions against societies and still more withheld mortgage payments until the outcome was determined. At one point a "National Federation" was formed to co-ordinate their claims. In the end Mrs Borders was unable to prove that the society was responsible for the contents of the brochure, or that the mortgage was unenforceable as a result of the builders' deposit; but the episode revealed a deep-seated hostility to the mechanism of house purchase on the part of a large number of people. At one point Mrs Ellen Wilkinson, the well-known Labour politician, introduced a bill into the Commons which would have had the effect of making building societies responsible for the quality of materials and workmanship in houses for which they provided mortgages; but the government was already preparing its own bill and the Wilkinson measure did not proceed.

The 1939 Act, drawn up and passed in the shadow of the war and the Borders' case, was a measure quite distinct from previous building society legislation in that it concerned itself in a knowledgeable way with the detailed business of the movement. It limited collateral security in such a way as to make the operation of a "builder's pool" an expensive matter for the builder (so much so that the institution withered and died); made it an offence to represent the willingness of a society to lend on a dwelling as evidence of its value; put an end to the practice (common with some societies) of selling houses possessed through default back to builders at lower than market prices, and made commissions paid to any person having an interest in the sale of property unlawful.

So strongly was public opinion running against the alliance of builders and societies at the time that an amendment requiring the societies to guarantee the reasonableness of the purchase price of houses bought with the aid of builder's deposits was only defeated by the casting vote of the chairman in standing committee; while a clause insisting that societies certified the quality and habitability of the house before issuing the mortgage was carried against the government, though it was later deleted.[1]

What the effect of market saturation in the late 1930s, allied to public displeasure and the provisions of the 1939 Act, might have been without the outbreak of war is difficult to determine. The societies themselves were in many cases dangerously low on non-mortgage assets, but small withdrawals accompanying the Munich crisis of 1938 enabled them to take action in time to forestall the more serious run which began in 1939; and with the fall of France in 1940 the government stepped in, requiring six months notice of withdrawal under Defence Regulations.

But by the year 1940 the problem of assets and withdrawals in the building society movement had ceased to be of great concern to householders of any description, much less to the government. The war itself had intervened in the most direct and destructive manner.

Aerial bombardment had of course been a factor in the Great War, but its effects had been minute compared to the visitation of 1940. From the defeat of France until the Normandy landings 126,000 houses were destroyed and of the million or so damaged, 150,000 still remained derelict at the latter date. With the invasion of continental Europe the flying bomb offensive began and even more serious harm was done. In one London suburb during August 1944 as many as 20,000 houses a day were being damaged and by October 23,000 more houses had been completely destroyed and 1.1 million damaged. By the end of the war 200,000 houses had been wiped out, 250,000 so badly hit that they were evacuated, and over three million listed with the War Damage Commission as having sustained injury of some kind.

These successive waves of physical damage, combined with the enormous organisational changes brought about by the war itself, created considerable uncertainty. During the war there were 60 million changes of address in a population of 38 million: more than five million men and women were drafted into the armed services, and millions more registered for national service and were relocated according to the needs of food and war production. Under emergency legislation protection was granted to mortgage holders and rent payers whose financial position was seriously affected by war damage or war work, and as a consequence

[1] Cleary (*op cit*) page 221.

rumours abounded that there was a moratorium on mortgage debts. Arrears rose rapidly, from £1.1 million in 1939 to £11 million in 1942, partly as a result of uncertainty about the position of bombed-out mortgage holders, who were generally required to maintain 5% of their mortgage payments until the end of the war, when it was promised that they would be compensated at 1939 values plus 2½% interest from the date of destruction.[1]

Bomb damage sharpened the edge of the ruthless system of state controls inaugurated by the coalition government which took power in May 1940. Not only were the mechanisms developed in the Great War rolled into action again, but the coalition proved itself to be the greatest reforming administration since the Liberal government of 1905–14. Unprecedented measures in the fields of social security, family allowances, education, health care, full employment, town and country planning and (in the last phase) housing, created radical new perspectives for the future of the country.[2] That such measures were accepted without complaint speaks for the remarkable unanimity of purpose which characterised the time, and for the egalitarian manner in which Keynesian economics, price controls, subsidies, taxation and rationing were employed.

Economically it was clear to everyone (except perhaps the leader of that remarkable coalition) that there could be no return to the "good old days" at the end of the war with Germany. Not only was the loss of foreign resources and domestic capital during the struggle catastrophic, but the cost of the war over five years absorbed about half the current production of goods and services in Britain. By 1944 consumption had fallen 20% from 1938 even though incomes were 50% higher. Without a continuation of wartime controls the inflationary pressure on prices in 1945 would have been irresistible.

[1] In 1944 the Halifax, in a publicity move aimed at post-war business, reduced the percentage of the mortgage repayment payable on destroyed or uninhabitable houses to 2½% and made this retrospective to the date of the damage. This unilateral act was widely criticised by other societies, who were obliged to follow suit. Cleary (op cit) page 231.

[2] Paul Addison The Road to 1945: British Politics and the Second World War London 1975 makes the comparison with the pre-Great War Liberal government and develops the case for regarding the wartime coalition of 1940–45 as a more radical government than the Labour administration which followed it.

High wartime wages had also had an effect on savings institutions such as the building societies. In 1939 less than one million manual workers had paid income tax; by 1944 seven million paid regularly, and at rate nine times higher than in the last peacetime year. Government measures encouraged savings and, as soon as the wave of withdrawals which greeted the fall of France had been stemmed, the societies began to face the Great War problem of placing their own accumulating funds. This time there was no relief in government bonds, for high taxation and low interest rates threatened them with capital losses should they buy large holdings only for interest rates to surge after the war. After 1942 many societies actively discouraged new share or deposit accounts by reducing interest rates, while others invited mortgage holders irrespective of their circumstances to repay only the interest on their loans. When the societies were permitted to become agents for the sale of National Savings Certificates, they directed incoming funds into these and similar securities. Competition between societies for the small amount of mortgage business available during the war was intense and this, among other frictions, led to a period of amalgamation during which large societies began to absorb the small, local societies which had always predominated numerically, and the largest societies (such as the Abbey Road and the National) merged to produce organisations familiar in building society advertising today.

The government first announced the formation of a post-war reconstruction committee in January 1941 under the chairmanship of Arthur Greenwood, a former Labour Minister of Health; but the problem did not receive serious attention until a year later under the impact of Lord Beveridge's report on social services, when it became apparent that housing was high on the list of popular priorities.[1] In 1942 the Building Societies Association formed their own post-war reconstruction committee and, as a result of a series of conferences held in 1943 at which the Royal Institute of British Architects and the National House Builders'

[1] Addison (*op cit*) cites the June 1942 Ministry of Information report on public feeling over post-war issues which placed housing fourth, after full employment, curbing of profits, and unemployment benefits. By October 1944 Home Intelligence placed it second, after full employment. In the run up to the 1945 general election housing took first place, followed by employment and social security.

Registration Council were represented, issued a report in January 1944 which called for the construction of four million new houses after the war, most of them low-cost dwellings to let. To finance this programme the report suggested that the government revive the lapsed provisions of the 1933 Housing Act which had introduced a system of combined local government, central government and society guarantees for 90% advances to private developers: an arrangement which had not proved conspicuously productive, contributing only 17,000 dwellings by 1940.

Much of course depended on the political complexion of the post-war government, and in the event the only matter of agreement between the societies and Labour concerned tenure, for surprisingly both agreed that housing to let was of the highest priority. Otherwise there appears to have been no connection between the ideas of the building societies and the ideas of the government, even during the coalition period. All three of the major reports on issues affecting housing which were published during the war suggested government intervention on a scale non-existent during the boom years of the 1930s. The Barlow Report (1940) recommended government control of land use, redistribution of urban populations and location of new industry in areas of high unemployment. The Scott report on rural development, and the Uthwatt report on compensation and betterment (1942) both implied direct interference with property values, the latter in particular, although it did not accept the proposal that land as a whole should be nationalised, recommended the nationalisation of development rights. The building societies waited to see what action would be taken on thse matters before they committed themselves fully, and this reluctance played a part in their exclusion from the far reaching plans even then being drawn up.

At first the coalition government appeared to be excessively cautious with regard to post-war housing. The programme outlined by the Minister, Mr Willink, in March 1944 called for the completion of 100,000 permanent homes in the first year after the war and 200,000 in the next. In an open debate on housing held on 15th March the House of Commons expressed deep dissatisfaction with these inadequate measures and called for a properly thought out long term programme. At this Mr Churchill revealed his major strategy. In a broadcast one week later he not only announced a 12-year plan for the building industry to guarantee full employment, but gave the first details of a Ministry of Works project for "Emergency Factory Made Houses" (EFMs), of which he promised 500,000 immediately after the war. "The whole business," he explained, in the first of many encouraging parallels to be drawn between winning the war and solving the housing problem, "is to be treated as a military evolution handled by the government with private industry harnessed in its service. . . . As much thought will be put into the prefabricated housing programme as went into the invasion of Africa."

The EFM or "prefab" programme, as it came to be called, grew out of a number of wartime studies of which the Burt Committee Report on pre-war prefabrication methods (1943) and the work of the Building Research Station (which evaluated 1400 industrialised housing proposals by the end of 1945) are the best known. The Ministry of Works and Planning, formed in 1942, and the Ministry of Aircraft Production also sponsored studies and in March 1944 the former introduced an "experimental temporary bungalow" developed by the motor vehicle industry. The "Portal", as this house was called, after the Minister of Works, had a floor area of 616 square feet (one third larger than the minimum size laid down for subsidised housing in 1919) and was expected to cost £600 exclusive of £75 site preparation. Rapidly assembled and expected to last ten years, the "Portal" was to be let at a rent of ten shillings a week.

Here indeed was a "secret weapon" in the housing war, and the "Portal" was only the first in a generation of small prefabricated dwellings. The most sophisticated of all, the AIROH house,[1] scheduled to be built by the aircraft industry, was constructed of aluminium alloy and expected to roll off former bomber production lines at the rate of one every twelve minutes. In retrospect it is clear that the "prefab" programme was the nucleus of what might have developed into the most sophisticated housing policy ever proposed by a British government. Plans were made to employ airfield construction plant for site preparation, and the

[1] The initials stood for "Aircraft Industries Research Organisation on Housing." Though unprepossessing in appearance the AIROH was technically impressive, consisting of four 22ft 6in × 7ft 6in sections complete with decoration, furniture, plumbing and wiring, which were bolted together on site. The whole house weighed less than ten tons.

switch over from military production to housing production in the motor vehicle and aviation industries was intended to prevent the massive redundancies widely feared towards the close of the war. There was an irrefutable logic to this attempt to make good the ravages of bombing, scarcities and cost increases by drastically improved productivity, but alas the programme was beset by problems, not all of them technical.

Churchill's broadcast itself had not been as well received as was expected and much of the early publicity for the "prefabs" was poorly handled, with the result that it was widely believed that "Portal" houses were to be the permanent houses of the future: a belief which was for some reason peculiarly depressing. On 1st August a second reading of The Housing (Temporary Accommodation) Bill, which moved the funding of £150 million for the "prefab" programme, was refused as a result of objections by Members of the idea of thousands of "eyesores" dotted about the country. How far the alarm of the construction industry and allied institutions such as the building societies contributed to this unexpected hostility has never been determined. The state financed construction of half a million prefabricated dwellings a year, to be let at controlled rents and produced by labour not hitherto associated with building, was clearly a prospect of concern to those organisations which had traditionally dominated the housing market. The entire balance between existing stocks and annual production would have been upset, perhaps forever, had the "prefab" industry entrenched itself in the post-war years.[1]

With admirable determination the coalition persisted with its plans, but by the end of the year more fundamental problems had surfaced. In December the Ministry of Works confessed that shortages of labour and manufacturing facilities were delaying improvements to the "Portal" house. This, the first indication of trouble with what appeared to be the cheapest and best of the

[1] It is tempting to consider the parallel development of the mobile home industry in the United States, which grew from 37,000 completions in 1946 to over half a million annually by the early 1970s. The existence of such an industry in Britain would surely have eased the growth of unsatisfied demand at the lower end of the housing market in the 1960s.

"prefabs",[1] was not reflected in the White Paper on housing policy published in March 1945. In this document the first two years after the war were designated "emergency production years" during which the EFM programme was to play a key part in overall housing strategy, with the first 150,000 units being allocated to local authorities for emergency relief. In the longer term the government now committed itself to the construction of 750,000 new houses to "provide a separate dwelling for every family that desired one," together with another 500,000 to replace unfit housing and combat overcrowding. In the ensuing debate the Minister was closely questioned about the cost of the "prefabs" and he conceded that the projected figure for the "Portal" and the "Arcon" (an asbestos variant) was now £800 each, while the sophisticated AIROH had risen to £950.

Clement Attlee's Labour government, which won the general election of July 1945 with a large majority, inherited the "prefab" programme when it took office and presided over the last act of the drama. A government White Paper published in August confessed that the "Portal" house had been abandoned for lack of steel while the cost of other types of "prefab" had risen to £1270 for the "Arcon" and £1400 for the AIROH. This was a severe blow from which the programme never recovered: productivity could not compensate for such increases and in the end a bare 170,000 "prefabs" were built before all remaining orders were cancelled in 1947. It is a mute testimony to the value of the original idea that 30 years later thousands of them are still occupied.

At the time of the 1945 election campaign the failure of the EFM programme still lay in the future, but the issue of housing policy had already assumed the same overriding importance as in 1918. Public opinion sampling in the spring of 1945 showed that housing was now placed first, out of a whole range of post-war issues. Labour politicians instantly seized the initiative and talked (wildly, as it turned out) of the construction of four or five

[1]Lord Portal himself exerted a particularly unfortunate influence on the development of the house that bore his name. Dismayed by lack of public enthusiasm in 1944 he decreed that the cause lay in the design of the ground support system of the house, which lifted it above site level. Efforts to remedy this "defect" eventually increased the cost of the unit by nearly one third.

million houses in ten years; but the Conservatives shifted their emphasis to foreign policy to an extent that probably contributed to their failure. The sober truth was that there were categorical imperatives facing whichever party gained power that would determine the fate of any housing programme.

Notwithstanding Labour's concentration on domestic issues, it was evident that an increased share of the nation's output of goods would have to be diverted to exports so that the balance of payments could be restored. Lend-Lease, the wartime arrangement under which the United States had supplied Britain with food and raw materials in return for the allocation of greater resources to the war effort, ended abruptly with the defeat of Japan and had to be replaced by a hastily negotiated £937 million loan, which was to be repaid over fifty years starting in 1950. At the same time means had to be found to direct a larger proportion of the national income into investment, so as to improve productive efficiency. Together these two strategies would have to ensure survival, for the massive increase in public expenditure required by the unprecedented programme of social services promised by the Labour government alone guaranteed the continuation of high, wartime rates of taxation.

Whether the ultimate effect of these economic millstones was foreseen by the protagonists in the drama which was now to unfold is not recorded, but the Labour government began its housing programme boldly enough. The new Minister of Health, Aneurin Bevan, most of whose energies were absorbed by the creation of the National Health Service, spoke with determination on the subject of housing. "Just as when an airfield was needed there were no protracted negotiations with the landowner," he explained to the House of Commons in October 1945 "So we will have no protracted negotiations with landlords for getting houses." He was as good as his word, and over the next five years a flurry of drastic measures flowed from a government determined to undo the misery caused by the unfulfilled promise of inter-war administrations.

Rent controls, which had been frozen at 1939 levels early in the war, were renewed indefinitely. The contentious Uthwatt report was translated into legislation in the Town and Country Planning Act of 1947, which not only made all land subject to planning schemes for the first time, but imposed a 100% development levy on the value created by permission to develop land. Amongst all the other nationalisation measures (the Bank of England, 1946; coal mines, 1947; electricity companies, 1948; gas companies, 1948; the railways, 1948; iron and steel, 1951), the nationalisation of land itself was annually proposed but rejected, though only for reasons of "administrative complexity." The actual housing programme itself was (after the demise of the "prefab" plan) almost exclusively a local government responsibility, controlled by the Ministry of Health—which was allegedly issuing six housing directives every week by 1946. Considerable subsidies were offered to offset the high cost of buildings so that the resultant dwellings could be let at controlled rents and the local authorities themselves were able to borrow money over 60 years from a Public Loans Board at an effective 3% interest.

The actual allocation of building resources, labour and materials, was controlled by an extension of the system of building licencing introduced during the war. Under local authority control this measure severely restricted private development and it was not until 1948 that any fixed allocation for private building was granted, and then it was limited to 20% of all housing built by the authority. Such private building as did take place was also restricted by cost limits (to ensure that only small houses were built) and a restraint on resale for four years. Local authorities were provided with funds for the purchase of owner-occupied houses for letting, and were also empowered to loan on mortgage in their own right.

Had the development of exports and investment in productive efficiency gone according to plan, it is possible that a very high housing output might have resulted from these draconian methods. As it was results even before the "Winter Crisis" of 1947 were disappointing. Between April 1945 and July 1946 only 60,452 new local authority dwellings were completed, two thirds of them "prefabs"; although over 100,000 badly damaged houses were repaired and reoccupied and 34,000 private houses had been built by the end of 1946. The cruel winter of 1946–47 finally spelled the ruin of the programme for by February transport was paralysed and electricity generation faltered through lack of coal, trapped immovably at the pits. 1947 housing targets, which had called for 240,000 permanent houses and 60,000 "prefabs"—of which total only 35,000 were to be built by private enterprise—had been based on the allocation of 62% of all construction and engineering resources to house building. The winter rendered this impossible. Worse still, of the 1946 American loan only £250 million was left, and the crisis of convertibility which arose when for five weeks in the summer of 1947 the government was forced to redeem its wartime borrowings in dollars, cost the Treasury 84% of its dollar reserves.[1] The British gross national product, worth sixteen times the 2400 million dollar reserve held in the spring of 1947, proved inadequate to support sterling; so yet more of the country's resources had to be thrown into capital investment and export.

It may not be immediately obvious why this economic crisis, which eventually culminated in the 31% sterling devaluation of 1949 and the progressive disintegration of the sterling trade area thereafter, should have so gravely affected the Labour government's housing programme. But the connection is direct and (as we shall see) not without its relevance today. Britain had been virtually bankrupted by "one war too many" and the only credit in the national account was British productive capacity, which could turn imported raw materials into manufactured goods to be sold abroad. All labour and material diverted to housing was lost to the export drive; furthermore housing (particularly conventional housing) was labour intensive and a prime consumer of strategic raw materials such as timber. After 1947 it was impossible to pretend that national economic survival could be combined with the development of a massive publicly-owned housing programme, which used national resources to subsidise both construction costs and rents. Labour's ambitious housing plans failed because in the ultimate analysis the priority enjoyed by

[1]During the war Britain had borrowed extensively from her dominions and colonies against the security of sterling notes. When exports began after the war these same notes were offered in payment, although the overwhelming need was for dollars to pay back the 1946 American loan whose terms required convertibility in 1947. Until July 1947 the British government was able to prevent the conversion of these sterling notes into dollars and, when faced with disaster after five weeks of convertibility, did so again until the devaluation of 1949. But the operation of the "dollar pool" was a rearguard action in defence of sterling whose only hope of success lay in massive exports which failed to materialise.

housing itself—however high in the eyes of the Labour voters of 1945—was lower than that of economic survival.[1]

The whole thrust of Labour's housing effort, which by the time the party lost power in 1951 had produced one million dwellings, was towards the provision of housing as a social service at rents the poorest could afford. Comparisons between local authority and "prefab" housing output over the six years of Labour rule, and the output of the private sector alone over the six years leading up to the war frequently ignore this fact. Because Labour was endeavouring to *absorb* the massive increase in costs and demand that the war years had produced, it was engaged in a qualitatively different process than pre-war Conservative governments, whose only concession to such matters had been the reluctant maintenance of rent control.

If the private builder survived rather than thrived during Labour's term of office (only 250,000 private houses were built between 1939 and 1951), the building societies positively boomed. Whilst it had always been clear that there would be no place for them in government plans if Labour came to power after the war,[2] they nonetheless enjoyed a spectacular growth which began as soon as the war ended. Annual advances on mortgage, which had slumped to £10 million in 1941, increased by ten times in 1945 and leapt to £188 million in 1946. The source of this business was not new construction but a spate of sales from the private rental sector reminiscent of the first casualties of rent control in 1919. While the socialists were busy trying to turn the local authorities and New Town Commissions into large-scale public landlords, the bulk of the private landlords who had hung on to their "investments" through the war years now concluded that

[1]Or as the Labour Party itself put it four years later: "We are already using more of our national income on capital investment than before the war and we are spending a higher percentage of our net capital investment on housing than other European countries. If we decide to spend still more on housing it means cutting down either on capital investment such as new schools, new power stations and new factories, or else cutting down the general standard of living in the country and adding to the risk of inflation." *Facts and Figures for Socialists* 1951.
[2]As early as 1943 the socialist theoretician G. D. H. Cole, in discussing the formation of agencies for post-war housing, had dismissed the building societies as "part of a Conservative plot to hinder socialistic tendencies." *Architectural Design and Construction* December 1943.

rent control was a fixture, and loss-cutting sales to sitting tenants resumed in earnest. So too did the ingenious speculations surrounding the securing of vacant possession, only this time the building societies played a more imaginative part.

A characteristic of the abuses which had culminated in the "greatest crime of the 19th century" ("The Liberator" crash of 1892) had been the practice among building societies of making large loans to property companies. This practice resumed with a vengeance in the 1940s, though on a slightly different basis. In many cases it began with the formation of limited companies by the managers of building societies; these companies then purchased large blocks of rent-controlled property at low prices, using society advances, and resold the individual dwellings to sitting tenants at a profit. Since the societies also provided funds for these latter transactions, the limited companies could "arrange" enticingly high advances, often higher than the full purchase price. The extent of this practice was sufficient to be reflected in society returns to the Chief Registrar (since a condition of the 1894 Act had been the disclosure of all loans above £5,000), and between 1945 and 1948 large loans rose from 7% to over 9% of advances. Lack of vigorous protest ensured that this dubious activity continued until the inevitable explosion, which involved the jailing of the managing director of the State building society ten years later.

The enormous turmoil of the war and the changes wrought by the post-war Labour administration marked a turning point in the history of housing. The number of dwellings rented from local authorities doubled between 1945 and 1951 so that by the latter year two million houses (15% of the total stock in England and Wales) were publicly owned. From this point on the Labour party based its political support on local authority tenants while the Conservative party turned increasingly to the owner occupiers. In the struggle which followed, the private landlord, controller of nine out of every ten houses in the country only thirty years before, was to virtually disappear. No Party ever effectively spoke for private rental again.

6 Owner Wins

"If the provision of subsidised council housing is a social necessity forced on us by the technological development of the modern conurbation, the provision of houses for sale to the potential owner-occupier is a response to a deep call of human nature."

Richard Crossman MP, Minister of
Housing and Local Government 1965

Arnold Whittick, a prolific writer of architectural books, spent part of the Second World War lecturing to servicemen and women about housing in the future. An unashamed Modernist, he propagandised for flat roofs, large windows, dining kitchens, all-electric houses and other fashionable ideas; but at the close of each lecture he asked the audience a number of questions about their preferences and recorded their answers. One of the questions was "Would you rather rent or buy a house?"

In his account of the discussions surrounding this question, which he asked on eight occasions of an aggregate audience of 450 persons, Whittick notes[1] that to most people at that time "the only advantage of renting a house was one imposed by economic necessity" and consequently he found it impossible to discuss the matter without putting the question in two ways. "Would you rather rent or buy a house (a) assuming economic and social conditions to be those obtaining in the year 1938, and (b) assuming that you are assured in the future of a regular income sufficient to provide the necessities of life?" Under condition (a) 20% of his aggregate audience voted for rental, and under condition (b) 2%.

The results of this mini-survey are interesting, not merely

[1]Arnold Whittick *The Small House: Today and Tomorrow* London 1947. Appendix II "Accounts of discussions among men and women in the forces on types of housing that are wanted, and records of voting on these preferences."

because of the period in which it was made, but because of the importance attached by Whittick's citizen soldiers to full employment as a prerequisite to home ownership. Full employment had clearly not (as far as they were concerned) existed in 1938; nor had it existed before 1914. Between 1945 and 1951 there was undoubtedly full employment, but also active government discouragement to home ownership. In the next twenty years all their conditions were exceeded; there was continuous full employment and mounting support for home ownership on the part of virtually every organisation in any way connected with housing. The years 1951 to 1971 were a kind of golden age for owner-occupiers: gone was the uncertainty of the first half of the century —between 1914 and 1950 the country was at war for the equivalent of one day out of every three and a half—and still to come were the alarming cracks in the firmament of the 1970s. In an "affluent" society "divided not so much between 'haves' and 'have-nots' as between 'haves' and 'have-mores' "; where the "class escalators" were "continually moving"—to use the descriptors of a leading politician of the period[1]—the growth of home ownership and the happiness of home owners were equally evident.

The building society movement greeted the 1951 change of government with relief. Although its total assets had increased from £823 million to £1,357 million under socialist rule, its leaders had not enjoyed being described as "mere moneylenders" by the Minister of Health, nor had they viewed with equanimity the measures taken to permit the local authorities to make fixed-interest mortgages and borrow money at 3% from the Public Works Loan Board. The Conservative Party too was committed to a high level of house building, having set itself an election manifesto target of 300,000 completions a year, but it was clear from the very beginning that the shackles were to be struck from the limbs of the private sector in pursuit of this aim.

Between 1954 (when the last remants of building licencing were swept away) and 1957 (when the most determined effort to remove rent controls since their inception in 1915 reached the statute book) the new policy took shape. With growing confidence the Conservatives moved towards the ultimate goal of removing the government from housing altogether: for various reasons this

[1] R. A. Butler at the Conservative Party Summer School, July 1960.

was not achieved, but from the viewpoint of the owner occupier the effort was rewarding. The local authority building programme was first stabilised, then slowly cut back and switched to slum clearance; a repetition of the strategy pursued by pre-war Conservative governments. Houses requisitioned from landlords "after no protracted negotiations" by Labour after the war were either returned or purchased outright, while the local authorities themselves were slowly forced into the open money market and away from the Loan Board. Development charges, and the 100% levy on value increases resulting from permission to develop land had already been abolished in 1953. The societies' own pet project, restoration of the 1933 tripartite guarantee system to facilitate 90% mortgages, which had been proposed by their own wartime reconstruction committee and ignored by both Coalition and Labour governments, was approved by the Conservatives in 1954.

In the same year the new government fired the first shot in what was to become the most acrimonious housing issue of the decade. The Housing Repairs and Rents Act marked the beginning of a battle fought not so much for the private landlord, as over his dead body. Under the Act private landlords were permitted to increase rents above controlled levels where they could show that repairs and modernisation had been carried out, and also to increase rents to compensate for increases in costs over 1939 levels on tenancies made since that date. Since at that time about half the housing in England and Wales was privately let, the un-impressive results of this measure convinced the Conservatives that they had simply not gone far enough. They thus began to frame a more comprehensive decontrolling measure, which was to emerge as the 1957 Rent Act.

The response of the Labour Party to the 1954 Act was to propose the municipalisation of all privately tenanted property—in effect the compulsory purchase of half the dwellings in the country. Public response was not encouraging; the time for such drastic measures had passed and in the general election of 1955 the socialists lost again with a fall of nearly 3% in their vote. The way was now clear for the final removal of rent controls, which had by then been in operation (with minor revisions) for 40 years, and in consequence much optimism was expressed about the recuperative powers of private landlords.

The 1957 Rent Act was introduced on the grounds that rent control caused under-occupation, restricted mobility, prevented new building for rent and prevented existing landlords from adequately maintaining or improving their property. The proposed answer was progressive decontrol of rents and an end to the security of tenure which discouraged both low-income letting to lodgers and new building. The Labour Party painted a Dickensian picture of the probable consequences; savage rent increases, cruel evictions and widespread hardship. The actual results were to disappoint both parties.

Rateable values had last been established in 1938 and the 1957 Act was limited in its application to dwellings above a certain rateable value: the Ministry of Housing (successor since 1951 to the department of the Ministry of Health formerly responsible for housing) anticipated that about eight million dwellings would be decontrolled, but in fact less than half this number were above the value established by the Act. Rent increases too were lower than expected, rising only 19% on average by 1962. But the worst miscalculation concerned the nature of the private landlord himself who, far from seizing the opportunity created for expansion and improvement, merely used the provisions of the Act to obtain vacant possession and sell.[1] Whether he was influenced in this by the socialist threat to repeal the Act once Labour regained power is not clear, but the Greve survey,[2] carried out five years later, went far to dispel the illusions about wicked landlords so sedulously maintained since 1914.

---

[1]Opinions about this differ. L. J. Macfarlane (*Issues in British Politics Since 1945*) claims that the Act actually decreased the number of dwellings sold out of private rental, whilst conceding that 300,000 privately rented dwellings were lost between 1958 and 1964 and quoting Grevé (*op cit*) on the ratio of one sale out of every three vacancies. Berry (*op cit*) clearly states that the Act "increased dramatically" the number of houses sold out of rental "by perhaps as many as 100,000 a year." Using figures for the growth of owner-occupation coupled with figures for the construction of new houses, it is clear that about 1,150,000 dwellings came into owner-occupation from sources other than new building between 1938 (Fitzgerald *op cit*) and 1961 (*Census Housing Report*). These must have come from the private rental sector after 1945, perhaps in two spurts; the first 1945–49, the second 1957–61.

[2]John Greve *Private Landlords in England* Occasional Papers on Social Administration No 16 (Bell 1965).

According to Greve only 5% of landlords owned more than 10 tenancies, and of those few with more than 100, over 50% had been in their hands since before the Great War. Of these "large" landlords none had invested in new lettings since 1950. The overwhelming majority of landlords were old or retired persons who "belonged to another time and different circumstances," and on average one out of every three of their dwellings was sold on becoming vacant. The Greve report merely confirmed what should have been obvious: there was no way that this obsolete form of tenure could be resuscitated. The numerical supremacy of private rental was of no importance because it masked a disorganised, impoverished and chronically under capitalised band of old-age pensioners.

The Conservatives learned the lesson of the 1957 Act with remarkable speed and turned immediately to the support of owner-occupiers with two unconnected but nonetheless unequivocal measures, both designed to ensure that owner-occupiers would henceforth connect their good fortune with the benign policies of the Party. Early in 1958 consultations were held with the Building Societies Association in an endeavour to increase the supply of mortgage funds for older houses: exactly the type so frequently made vacant in the private rental sector. The upshot of these talks was a government proposal for the loan of £100 million to the societies at $\frac{1}{2}$% below the rate paid to ordinary depositors; the money was to be used for mortgages on houses built before 1919 which would henceforth be offered at up to 95% of valuation. This arrangement was codified in the 1959 Housing and House Purchase Act and bore immediate fruit, the societies borrowing £8 million in the year of the Act, £37 million in 1960 and £47 million in 1961 when adverse economic circumstances caused the government to suspend the scheme.

The second measure followed immediately upon the heels of the first. In his budget speech in 1962 the Conservative Chancellor announced the impending removal of Schedule A income tax for owner-occupiers, which took effect the following year. Since it had been argued that the tax concession to building society borrowers on the interest included in their repayments was already an unfair advantage over the tax position of other householders, the removal of Schedule A tax seemed clearly to be preferential treatment. Schedule A tax itself had been a part of income tax since its

inception in 1842, being calculated on the income gained by
landlords from their tenancies according to the current rate assessment. Since, as we have seen, the rate schedule in effect in 1957
had not been changed since 1938 (with the anticlimactic effect on
the Rent Act already noted) measures had been taken to revise it,
and it was the scale of the emerging revision which had alarmed
the government. Rather than confront home owners with swingeing
increases in a tax designed to reflect the use-value of their own
dwellings, the Conservatives decided instead to remove the tax
entirely.[1]

Nothing more clearly indicates the importance which both
political parties now attached to the owner-occupier than the
failure of the Labour Party to react to, and the inequity of the
Conservative Party in resorting to this expedient. As P. R. Kaim-
Caudle wrote angrily in the March 1964 issue of *Local Government
Finance*:

"A man who invests £5000 in ordinary shares and receives £300
in dividends is liable to income tax in respect of this income.
Similarly a man who buys a house for £5000 and lets it at a net
rent of £300 is liable to tax on that amount. But a man who buys
a house for £5000 and occupies it himself, that is, receives in kind
a value equivalent to the £300 he would have received had he
chosen to let it, is now not liable to pay any tax at all."

From this point onwards both major parties competed in proposing
measures to win the votes of owner-occupiers as well as increase
their numbers. Despite the injustice to private landlords of the
Schedule A tax removal (local authority tenants had of course never
been taxed in this way) the Labour Party made no effort to

---

[1] The income tax concessions enjoyed by societies apply to both borrowers
and investors and date from the assumption made at the introduction of
income tax (in 1842) that all building society members earned less than
£150 a year—the lower limit for taxation purposes. With the growth of
the societies, efforts were made to apply tax to investors' dividends and
in 1894 agreement was reached that borrowers would pay no tax on the
interest element in their repayments, provided tax was paid by the
societies on half the sum distributed in interest payments to investors.
Modifications to this arrangement were made in 1916, 1921, 1925 and
1932.

reintroduce it, probably because the 1957 Rent Act had shown that the private rental sector was more realistically regarded as a reservoir of potential council tenants and owner-occupiers than as a form of tenure in its own right.

The effect of this avalanche of unintentional and intentional benefits upon the building societies was spectacular. During the thirteen years of Conservative rule their financial situation was transformed. At the beginning the total assets of the movement stood at £1357 million and annual advances were running at about £270 million a year. The total number of current mortgage holders stood at 1.58 million and the average advance was just under £900. By 1964, when the Labour Party again came to power, total assets had more than tripled to £4862 million and annual advances had increased by nearly four times to £1042 million. The number of current mortgage holders had almost doubled to 2.75 million and the average advance had more than doubled to £1948. The latter figure reflected a considerable increase in construction costs which was to play an even larger part in years to come, for the stability created by a depressed economy and low wage rates in the 1930s, and by high public and private sector output in the 1950s, was soon overtaken by demand in the next decade.

Unfortunately expansion was once again accompanied by abuses and, as before, these culminated in scandals and further legislation. The formation of property companies by the directors of building societies and its obverse, the formation of building societies by the directors of property companies, had begun in the years after the war. During the property boom of the 1950s the practice expanded and, because it was profitable, began to attract attention to itself with spectacular deals. Since the company in the partnership generally raised short-term loans to finance purchase of various kinds of property, then immediately repaid the loan by mortgaging the purchase to the society, the weak link in the chain was the ability of the company to raise capital. Here rising property values and the apparent formality of the transaction bred complacency. The State Building Society, with assets of only £½ million in 1952, increased them to £14 million seven years later, by which time it was advancing money to its associate property company *before* purchase. In July 1959 the society sent a cheque for £3.25 million to its own solicitors in connection with a massive takeover bid for the Lintang property company. Another £13 million was necessary to complete the deal and the company failed to obtain it: the State society was left with no property as security for its £3 million cheque.

The Lintang affair was a spectacular example of the interaction between the glamour world of the property companies at the height of their boom (when Lintang was floated in March 1959 queues of brokers pushed its ten shilling shares to twenty-two shillings within minutes) and the apparently more staid but often equally racy activities of the building societies. In the State catastrophe a kind of flash bulb illuminates the manner in which, notwithstanding the provisions of the 1894 and 1939 Acts and the watchful supervision of the Chief Registrar, some societies at least were operating along the perilous lines of "The Liberator" seventy years before.

There were indeed building society failures in the 1950s, but so large were the reserves of the movement and so eager for expansion were its member societies that none of them involved investors or borrowers in loss. The Exeter Benefit Society in 1956 and the Scottish Amicable Society in 1958 both invested their funds so unwisely that, at current market prices, their losses were not covered by their reserve funds: in both cases (as with the State society itself) other societies took over their commitments and the reputation of the movement did not suffer.

As previously in building society history, legislation followed swiftly upon scandal. No sooner had Mr Murray, the managing director of the State, been sentenced to five years imprisonment than the 1960 Building Societies Act became law. Its provisions ensured that no more than 10% of any societies' advances could exceed £5000 and that the formation of new societies was made considerably more expensive: for hitherto directors of property companies had frequently formed societies and advertised for funds to finance their own speculations. At the same time the Chief Registrar reserved the right to prevent societies from advertising if their returns appeared suspicious in any way, and to control the investment of surplus funds. An effective provision terminated the practice of society managers making their own valuations within ten years of the passage of the Act, and ensured that all loans from societies to their own officers should be identified in returns to the Chief Registrar's office: both of which struck at the heart of the abuses involving the simultaneous operation of societies and property companies for the benefit of their directors rather than investors in the society.

By the end of their long term of office, which came with Labour's victory in the October 1964 general election (their hopeful slogan "Britain belongs to you" had served them ill in the 1959 contest), the Conservative Party had ceased to believe that it could extricate government from housing altogether. Demographic realities, notably in the matter of accelerating rates of household formation and intolerable pressure on urban housing (compounded by slum clearance and redevelopment by local authorities at low densities), had convinced them that high public expenditure was essential to secure the social stability upon which the private sector rested. The Housing Act of 1964 reflected this change of heart by enabling local authorities to take over whole areas of unfit dwellings for compulsory management and improvement; but at the same time it created a new government agency, the Housing Corporation, which was to facilitate the construction of dwellings for rent and co-ownership by Housing Societies, using finance from government and building society sources combined. This much vaunted "Third Arm" of the housing drive was destined to play a disappointing part under both Labour and Conservative administrations in the future, although it was widely believed by the former that the Conservatives intended it as a means of eventually taking over the local authority role in the provision of new housing.

The enthusiasm of the Labour Party for long-term economic planning and advanced building technology had not been dimmed by their long period in opposition. After introducing their promised revision of the 1957 Rent Act—which created Rent Assessment Committees to oversee the activities of Rent Officers, themselves charged with the establishment of registered "fair rents" for all previously controlled tenancies besides requiring court orders for all evictions and making the harrassment of tenants a crime—they turned their attention to the impressively named "National Plan" in which housing was to play a major part. Ironically the provisions of the 1965 Rent Act were to return to haunt the socialists six years later, but the plan itself was destined to be soon forgotten.

The 1965 "National Plan" proposed annual 5% increases in housing output so as to achieve 500,000 houses a year by 1970, thus erasing once and for all the "absolute shortage" of 700,000 dwellings as well as the similar number of unfit dwellings enumerated by the Central Housing Advisory Committee. To help this ambitious programme cheap local authority borrowing was restored by a re-arrangement of housing subsidies so as to create an effective interest rate of 4% over sixty years. At the same time increasing use was to be made of new techniques in industrialised building, as was being done all over Europe. The plan foresaw an increase in approved tenders for industrialised building of over 250%, from 38,000 in the year of the plan to 100,000 in 1970. Because the economics of industrialised building required consistent high level demand, special consortia of local authorities were organised. It was in any case assumed that most of the increased housing output would be in the public sector for, as the plan succinctly put it "Many people want houses to rent, and it is the supply of rented houses which is totally inadequate. These will in present circumstances only be provided to any significant extent by the public authorities."[1]

For a time the heady days of the "prefab" programme returned, with the specially created National Building Agency evaluating over three hundred prefabricated building systems. But history was to repeat itself more accurately still. Exactly twenty years after the balance of payments crisis of 1947 (which had wrecked the housing plans of the 1945–50 Labour administration) another economic crisis forced a second devaluation of the pound. Austerity returned with a vengeance and the "National Plan" swiftly faded into oblivion, taking with it massive investment in preparations for industrialised building (itself somewhat discredited one year later by the partial collapse of a tower block in East London) and all prospect of record housing output in the 1970s. As a final blow the estimate of the number of unfit houses made by the Advisory Committee was challenged by the results of a National House Condition Survey carried out by experienced public health inspectors, who found not 700,000 slum dwellings but nearly two million.

It was at this point in a largely unexpected housing crisis that media interest in homelessness and bad housing conditions coincided with the reappearance of the spirit of 19th-century

[1] *The National Plan* Cmnd 2764, HMSO 1965, page 172.

philanthropy in the form of SHELTER and other less prominent housing trusts operated by young and zealous personalities eager for a place in public life. SHELTER hung like an albatross around the neck of Labour's luckless housing administration, constantly bringing its shortcomings to the attention of a now largely suburban public by means of dramatic fund-raising campaigns.

Like the Conservatives after the failure of the 1957 Rent Act to revive the private rental sector, the Labour Party reacted swiftly to the demise of their plans for new construction. As in 1947 expenditure on housing was hamstrung by the economic consequences of rising imports and falling exports, so instead of new building and comprehensive redevelopment (which had in truth destroyed vast areas of cheap urban accommodation and created intolerable pressure on that which remained) emphasis was shifted to rehabilitation. In their 1968 White Paper *Old Houses into New Homes* the government proposed that existing improvement grants should be greatly increased and made available to local authorities and individual householders for the comprehensive improvement of whole areas at, it was hoped, considerable savings to the exchequer. At the same time owner-occupation amongst lower income groups was to be encouraged by an option mortgage scheme (which would offer house buyers with earnings too low to benefit from mortgage interest income tax allowances a 2% lower interest rate), and by a guarantee scheme to permit 100% mortgages.

In the event the first of these innovations was to prove a greater boon to aspiring owner-occupiers than the second, for the option mortgage scheme was severely limited by the small number of house buyers who fell into the income bracket expected to benefit. Improvement grants on the other hand went on to become something of a scandal in later years for their enormous cost as well as their use to promote the "gentrification" by owner occupation of formerly working class urban areas.[1]

---

[1]Writing in *The Daily Mirror* in July 1968 Frank Allaun, Labour MP for East Salford, enthused, "Many realistic councils have taken advantage of the grant system. The difference between the cost of a new council flat at, say, £4,000, and a new bathroom at £400 is startling." Equally

Throughout the 1960s the accelerating increase in housing costs of all kinds which was to become a scandal in the following decade, played an important part in the growth of owner-occupation. While rising costs created political problems for the public rental sector and great hardship in the private rental sector, owner-occupiers found that the value of their dwellings acted as a hedge against inflation. Thus the doubling of the average building society advance between 1960 and 1970 (which of course reflected higher house prices) by no means discouraged would-be owners. Real disposable income in Britain rose by over 50% from 1950 to 1970 and with it the number of current mortgage holders. In 1951 just over 300,000 borrowers took an average of £890 in mortgage loans from the societies; in 1970 no less than 550,000 borrowed an average of £3500. In 1970 the number of mortgage holders was 250% higher than twenty years before, standing at a record 3.65 million. The total assets of the building society movement in the same year reached £11,000 million, a figure in excess of the assets of the clearing banks and vastly larger than those of any other savings institution.

As soon as the priority of housing fell in 1967 increasing attention began to be devoted to the exchequer subsidies paid to local authorities to augment their rent income from existing publicly rented housing. In the financial year 1966–67 rents produced £315 million, or 74% of total housing expenditure; and the evidence of former years suggested that this proportion had been steadily increasing since 1951. Unfortunately the burden of interest payments had been increasing too, so that whereas in 1960 only 50% of housing expenditure had been on loan servicing, by 1972 it had risen to 76%. Trapped by irreducible space standards (made mandatory in 1969 but adopted long before) and rigorous cost controls introduced in 1967, the public sector was running

startling perhaps was the eventual cost of the scheme. As Berry (*op cit*) notes, "Over the two-year period 1970–72 the cost of improvement grants increased by 440 % . . . the cost of improvement grants at the moment of writing (May 1974) could be running at something over £400 million a year. Compare this with the figure of £300 million a year which was held to be totally unacceptable as a level of subsidy to council building . . . All this money and not a single new dwelling to show for it." But of course the "right" people were receiving improvement grants, and the "wrong" people the housing subsidy.

out of funds for new construction, maintenance, and everything else except the payment of interest on sixty-year loans.

This crisis, already brewing in 1967, had been temporarily submerged by the effective 4% borrowing rate for local authorities created by the Housing Subsidies Act of the same year, but the high cost of local authority building remained a serious political issue which could only be resolved by increased subsidies or increased rents, or both. While Labour pondered these unpalatable alternatives, a surprise victory by the Conservatives in the general election of June 1970 took the matter out of their hands.

With refreshing political realism the new government endorsed home ownership as the central goal of housing policy. The problem of the essential role of the public sector, which had given the Conservatives such difficulty before 1964, was to be solved by two new measures: the sale of local authority housing to tenants, and the extension of Labour's own 1965 "Fair Rents" machinery to cover public sector rental as well as private. The sale of council houses had been presaged during Labour's own period of office by pilot schemes carried out by Conservative controlled local authorities,[1] but the inspired *detournement* of the provisions of the 1965 Rent Act was entirely new in that it enabled the Conservatives to usurp much socialist thinking on the allocation of housing subsidies to specific households rather than over the whole area of local authority housing. The new housing policy proposed to create what was in effect one aggregate rental sector out of the previously separate public and private rental tenures; henceforth subsidies would be calculated on an individual tenant basis across the whole spectrum of tenancies. Labour's painfully accumulated 4.5 million "privileged council tenants", the nucleus of the Party's electoral support, were to be progressively whittled away by the remorseless process of sales to sitting tenants which had successfully dismantled the initially much larger private rental sector. By this means the intolerable problem of loan repayments

[1] A Conservative Party Political Broadcast in March 1967 featured several tenants and their families from Birmingham City Council estates who had bought their houses at a discount. They all used phrases like "We had been waiting all our lives . . . It was a lifelong desire . . . It was our last chance . . . It was almost too late," to describe the purchase of dwellings they had, in most cases, been occupying for more than twenty years with full security of tenure.

and maintenance was to be lifted from the shoulders of the local authorities "at a stroke."

This spectacular policy, comparable only to the Labour Party's drastic extension of local authority power over house construction in 1945, was enshrined in the Housing Finance Act of 1972, a measure so bitterly fought by the Labour Party that at one time 17 local authorities declared that they would not put it into operation. In the form contemplated the Act was to steadily increase the rents paid by local authority tenants to an agreed "fair rent" level by increments of 50p per week. For those who could not afford "fair rents" rebates would be paid on an individual basis, a method likened by opponents to the "means test" welfare payments of the Great Depression.

Since the proposals of the Housing Finance Act were never fully put into operation, and indeed with the fall of the Conservative government in February 1974 were shelved indefinitely, it is possible to look at the entire housing policy of the 1970 Conservative administration as an historical phenomenon. No previous programme had ever demonstrated so clearly the triumph of owner occupation over all other forms of tenure. Quite apart from its effects on housing subsidies and rental income the operation of the Housing Finance Act would clearly have squeezed the previously inviolate public rental sector so as to produce a surge in demand for home ownership. Research indicated[1] that of the seven million tenants (public and private) in England and Wales, no less than 1.1 million could afford to buy with the aid of 100% mortgages (introduced by Labour in 1968) or the new "Low-start" mortgage scheme proposed in 1972. These tenants were to be the targets for local authority sales and new private building. In the fullness of time perhaps another million tenants would become

[1] Two reports commissioned by the Housing Research Foundation (an offshoot of the National Housebuilders Registration Council, itself an organisation representing "all officially recognised bodies concerned with new housing, including the National Federations of Building Trades Employers and Operatives, the Building Societies Association, the Royal Institute of Chartered Surveyors, the Royal Institute of British Architects and local authority associations") covered this area in 1970 and 1971: *Methods of Encouraging Home Ownership: a preliminary international survey* (1970) and *The Renter Prospects: a survey of householders who rent but could afford to buy* (1971). The second provided the estimate quoted.

co-owners through Housing Corporation financed schemes ranging from self-build projects to sitting tenant purchases of shared houses and apartment buildings. The enormous popularity of home ownership itself would have ensured that no bitterness attended these transformations; but just as surely Labour's political power would be destroyed.

By 1972 it must have appeared that everything was falling into place; tax relief on mortgage interest, freedom from capital gains tax and the coming removal of stamp duty on mortgages, all confirmed the privileged status of home owners—as in another way did rapid increases in house prices. At the same time remorselessly rising rents and declining standards of management and maintenance drove tenants to buy whenever they could: particularly in the public sector where a chill wind of change was shaking the previously complacent "working class aristocracy" from their torpor. By 1971 census figures showed that 52% of the 17 million households in England and Wales were owner-occupied; a crucial political majority. Soon an intelligent complicity with the economic forces now unleashed would force this percentage to 60, 70, or even higher. The economic burden of public housing would diminish and local authority spending on new housing would slowly merge into a matter of the administration of improvement grants and Housing Corporation projects, both speeding the transfer of yet more dwellings into private ownership.

The Minister for Housing and Construction, Mr Julian Amery, captured the moment perfectly when in July 1971 he addressed the annual conference of the National Housebuilders Registration Council, itself in the process of launching "Please the Customer Year."

"There is," he said, "no more worthy aim for any man than to own his own home. A home is not only the biggest investment most people make. It is also the best. What better to invest in than a home which will certainly appreciate in value and will, at the same time, give a man a feeling that there is a bit of England which is his family's own. And you have a government today which not only believes in the principle of owner-occupation but backs up its words with actions ... Once we have cured the nation's economic ills and got firmly on the road to real growth again, we shall see a new national spirit. In that fresh climate, home ownership will flourish. It will be re-endorsed as the primary aim of those who today cannot, or think they cannot, achieve it."

Mr Amery had made mistakes before: he had at one time advocated the loan of atomic bombs to Chiang Kai Shek in his battle with Mao Tse Tsung; but nobody imagined that there was anything wrong with his judgement on this occasion.

Part Three
Life in the Fast Lane

7 The Gazumpers

"How much do you owe on your mortgage? Now how does it compare with the present value of your home? The difference could mean a very useful source of credit. Say you owe £5000 on your mortgage, and your home is currently valued at £8000. We can help you turn a lot of that £3000 into cash. *Ready* cash instead of a locked up investment. It's well worth considering if you own your own home, especially with the terms that UDT Key Loan offers. The amount—anything from £350 to several thousand pounds. And it's yours fast."

United Dominions Trust
advertisement, June 1972

"The most far-sighted and courageous housing policy yet seen in this country," as the Conservative programme was described in *The Times* of 7th September 1970, got off to a good start. Despite the conclusion of the *National Westminster Bank Review* that rising mortgage interest rates had halved the number of households able to afford to buy a home since 1964, funds pouring into the building societies and rising incomes gave promise of revived sales. In July Mr Peter Walker, the new Minister of Housing and later first Minister for the Environment, not only initiated urgent talks with builders and the building societies designed to increase housing output, but also served notice that "fair rents" or not the Conservative Party proposed to have little to do with private landlords. Visiting two overcrowded houses in Brixton he emerged black with rage and declared to journalists, "All I can do is to express my complete disgust for any human being who exploits another human being in this way." One month later a luckless London landlady was jailed for illegally evicting the only tenant blocking vacant possession of her house.

"Help the home buyer" became the theme of government policy. Mr Walker was soon reported to be studying proposals for special low-start and lump-sum-at-termination mortgages which had appeared in the *Building Societies' Gazette*. In September Buckinghamshire County Council unveiled a range of "mini-homes" starting at £3500, fully mortgageable and "as cheap to own as a caravan." The Minister himself undertook a whistle-stop tour to promote improvement grants ("National home improvement week"), and announced that 17,000 grants were now being approved every month and 750 inquiries received every week by the Ministry alone. By the end of the year all parties concerned with home ownership were looking forward to a booming 1971. Building society net receipts had recovered strongly from £674 million in 1969 to £1213 million, and there was talk not only of record loans but even of cuts in the mortgage interest rate. Inspired by the shrewd observation of the property adviser to Hambro's Bank that the growth rate for property investment promised to be 13%—or 2% higher than that for Ordinary shares—institutions as well as individuals were acquiring property as fast as they could. Earnings had boomed in the late 1960s while house prices had increased by only 13% in three years. Revelations about the growth of homelessness and destitution provided the only dark side to the picture; in Manchester a Christmas celebration organised by young Quakers, offering food and shelter to the homeless over the holiday, failed to end on schedule because the beneficiaries had nowhere else to go.

In March 1971 the Conservative Political Centre produced a pamphlet entitled *Selling More Council Houses* which recounted in glowing terms the Party's achievements in Birmingham. In four years the Council had sold 5000 houses for a total of £12 million and was receiving inquiries at the rate of 400 a week.[1] The Greater London Council was also in business, not selling houses, but offering mortgages at 9¼% to 200 borrowers a week. A massively expansionist budget was greeted with mixed feelings by commentators, including Lord Balogh (a Cabinet adviser to the

---

[1] Sales of council houses in England and Wales peaked in 1972 at 45,878 dwellings, fell to 34,334 in 1973, fell again to 4,657 in 1974 and reached a five-year low at 2,723 in 1975. As can be seen from these figures, a considerable decline was evident before Labour suppressed the practice. The Conservative 1974 election promise of a one-third discount on market price might have revived sales had the Party been returned to power. Figures from *Housing and Construction Statistics No 20*.

previous government) who noted that the trend of unemployment was still rising, that production had fallen 4% in 1970 and was still falling, and that circumstances resembled a pre-war slump in all except rising prices. Builders too were worried about recession: fixed price tendering, in what was then described as a time of high inflation, had led to many bankruptcies during the credit squeeze and unemployment in the industry was still high. Despite the boom in house buying there was no comparable increase in new construction.

In the first half of 1971 house prices rose on average by 8% and a spokesman for the Nationwide building society predicted that the increase would continue "over the next five years." In August, long before the media caught on, SHELTER issued a statement deploring the abuses already current in the developing sellers' market. "Owners are holding out for inflated prices and getting them. Dutch auctions are being held in front rooms with buyers trying to outbid each other. Houses sold in the morning are withdrawn from deals in the afternoon as someone steps in and offers several hundred pounds more." Between January and June building society advances were up 37% on the same period in 1970, and the combination of improvement grants, pressure from fear of "fair rents" and a reduction in the borrowers' interest rate to 8% proved invincible as a stimulus to demand. The problem according to the National Association of Estate Agents was already a shortage of houses. In London a representative of the firm of Roy Brooks told the *Evening Standard* "People are desperate to get houses because they can't find what they are looking for. I tell them 'Get your foot on the ladder, whatever the price is.' " Although the national average house price at the end of the third quarter of 1971 was £6074 (6% up on the year's mid-point) the London average for a modest semi-detached was already £10,000. As a Kensington agent put it, "The country is geared to inflation. Everything else goes up, why not houses? Last year we were selling town houses for £25,000. Now they are around £30,000."

Towards the end of the year the most prevalent canard of the whole boom period surfaced for the first time. The Minister of Development was urged to demand that planning authorities produce, within six months, a list of sites available for development in 1972 over and above existing planning permissions. The theory that house production could solve the shortage and thus bring down the rate of increase in house prices, was rapidly transmuted into a theory of "land-hoarding" for which either "slothful" authorities or "speculators" were to blame. This theory was to be advanced and refuted repeatedly in the following year, although an alternative idea had already surfaced in an important pamphlet published during the summer[1] which argued that growth in real incomes was the most important cause of new household formation, and thus also underlay the continued and unforeseen demand for new housing.

By the close of 1971, despite a 40% increase in total advances (to nearly £2750 million) and a 20% increase in mortgage transactions, the net inflow of funds to the building societies had risen to £1700 million and their liquid assets were nearly 30% higher than at the beginning of the year. The ½% reduction in the mortgage rate (with a corresponding reduction in dividends) had not affected investment; nor had a 20% increase in average new house prices reduced demand—quite the contrary, as the very first day of the new year was to show, in an incident which was to feature in all daily newspapers, when more than twenty people celebrated the arrival of 1972 by queueing all night for twenty semi-detached bungalows and houses costing £8000 each. The houses, in Luton, Bedfordshire, were only half completed but the sales office was due to open at 10.30 on the morning of 1st January. Mr Gary Dalgleish, a 30-year-old metallurgist, had started the wait two days before. "I know it's ridiculous having to queue like this," he said, "but I have a new job in Luton and it's the only way."

In an equally alarming and characteristic incident a young couple who had paid a deposit on a £7500 house in the autumn of 1971, were notified by the estate agents in January 1972 that the price had risen to £9250. Their first reaction was to refuse to pay the increase and cancel the sale, whereupon the developer sold the house at the new price within 24 hours—before in fact the solicitors had returned the original purchaser's deposit.

---

[1]Colin Clarke and G. T. Jones *The Demand for Housing*, Centre for Environmental Studies 1971. The president of the Town and Country Planning Association described this report as "Dynamite beneath the preconceptions of British planners."

Questioned about the episode by the consumer services correspondent of a national newspaper, the developers (members of the National Housebuilders Federation) explained: "The fair price for a house is what the market will pay for it, and buyers found no difficulty in meeting the higher price that we charged."

In the first three months of 1972 a term once specific to the American used car market entered common British parlance. "Gazumping" in its original transatlantic sense meant the creation of imaginary competitors making imaginary offers to boost the price of a sale; in relation to the housing boom it retained this meaning (one could for instance be "gazumped" by a builder, an estate agent, or a private seller), but it also developed variations. A buyer might make offers on several properties only to withdraw all except one when he had determined which was the best prospect, and this too was called "gazumping." Worse still the seller or the seller's agent would wait until surveys had been carried out, loans obtained, every detail except the exchange of contracts finalised, before demanding the price increase. Under these circumstances the buyer was under the maximum possible pressure: house purchase usually takes months, and the thought of starting over again frequently squeezed more money out of the would-be owner than he or she had ever intended to pay in the first place. So great was public outrage at this practice that a private member's bill—the Gazumping and Kindred Practices Bill—was laid before parliament, but swiftly quashed through lack of parliamentary time. The bill in any case only proposed a four-week moratorium on price raising during sale negotiations, and could have been circumvented with ease.

By the end of March 1972 average house prices had risen by 8% in three months, with local increases, particularly in the London area, very much higher. A series of explanations for the unprecedented boom appeared in the press, most writers taking the view that a combination of factors was to blame. These included the willingness of the building societies to advance considerably more than in previous years; the rise in the price of land—either caused by hoarding or delays by local authorities in granting planning permissions; the shortage of houses to sell (*The Observer* noted that whereas the average estate agent had forty unsold houses on his books in November 1969, the number had fallen to eight by November 1971); the utterly inadequate number being built (this argument generally funnelled back into the land shortage cry); the unprecedented demand for home ownership, naively explained by a spokesman for the Abbey National building society as "More and more people want to be able to paint their front door whatever colour they please"; the failure of builders to respond to the sudden end of the 1968–70 credit squeeze (memories of bankruptcy were too powerful) and, finally, the accumulated effect of the credit squeeze and increasing incomes which had led to a distortion in the normal relationship between house prices and earnings. The latter theory, advanced with convincing economic data by *The Sunday Times* Insight Consumer Unit in April, triumphantly explained everything except the continuation of the phenomenon for another year and a half after parity had (apparently) been restored.

From diagnoses the commentators rapidly switched to remedies. Writing in the London *Evening Standard* Bennie Gray noted perceptively that the expansionist policies of the government, coupled with high interest rates, suggested that still more money would pour into the building societies. In order to "prevent this money fuelling the house-price spiral" he proposed freezing valuations (upon which mortgages are based) at the level of January 1972, and thereafter allowing them to rise only in response to increases in the cost of new building, rather than such leaps as the money-flooded market might permit. He then addressed himself to the nearly impossible task of determining the January 1972 value of all dwellings ("there would have to be some appeals machinery") and to controlling second mortgage companies ("the damage done would not bear comparison with the damage done by the house price spiral").

The Sunday Times Magazine took a different approach, with their leading assumption the not unreasonable one that the purpose of any regulatory legislation should be to "make home ownership easier." Controls on building society lending, whether direct or indirect (noted their writers), would undoubtedly slow down price rises but would also have an effect upon the owner-occupier market similar to that of rent control upon the private landlord. Their own remedies were designed to encourage first-time buyers at the expense of subsequent purchasers, and took the politically implausible form of a reintroduction of Schedule A income tax for home-owners, and the application of capital gains tax on profits from the sale of owner-occupied houses. Beyond this they could only point to the unfortunate effect of low output in the construction industry.

Letters following the *Magazine*'s marathon analysis contained more draconian but even less politically practicable ideas. One reader advocated massive tax abatements for the builders of "cheap flats and houses to let," a tax on the sale of houses within twelve months of purchase, repayable improvement grants and "an enormous tax" on empty dwellings. Another proposed a tax on under-occupation (to make more intensive use of existing housing), while a third advocated home extensions. There was predictable opposition to the reintroduction of Schedule A income tax and the levying of capital gains ("Why should a person who has practised thrift and made sacrifices to buy a house at penal rates of interest . . . be punished when he sells his property?")

The government's own response to the issue was characteristically robust. In March the National Economic Development Office released details of a new low-start mortgage scheme in which "a shift in the time pattern of payments would bring home ownership within the grasp of many tenants who are currently facing rent increases and are not eligible for rebate." While the Building Societies Association were still "expressing interest" in this project the Chancellor increased the exemption limit on stamp duty from £5500 to £10,000, an adjustment which meant that over 90% of all house purchases would escape duty altogether.

By the end of the second quarter of 1972 the average price of new homes had risen by more than 30% in a year (compared to 13% in the preceding three years) and matters were becoming much more serious. SHELTER's London Housing Aid Centre reported that "housing stress" now affected the ordinary family with average income, which could no longer find privately rented accommodation "as more and more landlords sell their property or convert it into 'luxury' flats," and had little hope of borrowing money to buy a £6500 house—now the minimum price in the London area. Less dramatic but politically more alarming signs began to be seen in the so-called "luxury" sector itself. On 8th April *The Times* ran a six-column front-page article on the "spectacle of middle-class couples camping on a building site in St John's Wood to queue for the privilege of paying up to £31,500 for a flat," and other atrocities of the booming property market.

Landlords, it appeared, were paying up to £2500 to induce "uneconomic" tenants to leave their apartments; buyers were faced with gazumpings of the order of 25% or more during negotiations; property companies were doubling "service charges" overnight and employing private detectives to uncover lease infringements which might provide grounds for eviction and subsequent sale at a profit. Hastily formed resident's associations had sprung up all over the city and their activities were to be coordinated by a London County Federation based in a flat in the 533 apartment Queen's Club Gardens, where the new owners, First National Finance Corporation, were creating alarm and despondency in their remorseless efforts to repossess and sell. "I do not believe in these financiers playing with homes like pawns in a game," the leader of the Federation was reported as saying. "We are not apples and vegetables to be bought and sold."

The shenannigans of the London luxury market offered an early insight into the massive shift in investment of which the house price surge was but one indicator. British property companies, always distinguished from their European and American counterparts by their system of valuations based on multiples of expected rent rather than construction costs, had grown and consolidated enormously despite the controls on new building enacted by the Labour Party on its return to power in 1964. By 1970 the largest quoted company, Land Securities and Investment Trust, owned properties valued at over £700 million and equities worth nearly half as much. Memories of the falling property values of the early 1930s had faded and increasingly insurance companies, pension funds and other institutions disposing of large investment assets had been making use of the imagined solidity of property holdings. Insurance companies alone had increased their investment in property from £63 million in 1963 to £186 million in 1969; while pension funds had boosted their own holdings by 500% over the same period. By 1972 insurance companies were pouring £250 million every year into property acquisition, while pension funds concentrated on the property unit trusts established to handle business from tax-exempt organisations including charities. In 1971 the net sales of these trusts exceeded £200 million.

Beyond these indirect routes to the property bonanza the public had shown increasing interest in property bonds, with a total investment in the 22 companies offering contracts in 1971 of another £200 million. More significantly still consumer credit, secured for the most part against the value of the homes of owner occupiers, rose by 36% from 1970 to reach £2740 million in 1971. The figure had doubled in four years. Starting in the summer of 1972 the finance houses began to lend heavily on appreciating home values with extensive advertising aimed at the mass market. United Dominions Trust for example, took half-page advertisements in national papers headlined "Cash in on the increasing value of your home without selling it." The Midland Bank's finance house subsidiary Forward Trust entered the booming second mortgage business in April 1972 in partnership with Guardian Guarantees, a subsidiary of the Vavasseur finance group. With money supplied by the Midland the new company proposed to spend nearly £½ million on advertising in its first year of operation.

These combined financial and social indicators confirmed the Conservative government in its "dash for growth" policy. Hardships created by the proposed "Fair Rents" Act, like the disturbances in the "luxury" rental sector and the apparent shortage of building land, were all seen as obstructions which entrepreneurial zeal would soon sweep aside. Massive increases in the money supply obscured falling industrial production and an alarming shift in investment away from the industrial sector altogether. For a time attention was focused on the myth of the "land hoarders."

As early as March *The Sunday Express* had used an urgent demand for more building land as a cover for disparaging comments on the Minister of Housing Mr Amery, who had apparently observed that while it was unfortunate that house-buyers should have to queue for houses in certain areas, it was "a good deal better to see this than the situation where people do not have the money and do not feel they can buy." In April the Conservative MP for Ipswich demanded that the three-year limit on planning permissions be cut to one year in order to stimulate new building, he also urged that undeveloped building land should pay a full rate for the same reason. An investigation carried out by *The Observer* revealed evidence of institutional involvement in land price gazumping, and a Surrey builder was quoted as saying "Speculation is a big problem, and I'm sorry to say that the speculators have been joined by insurance companies and merchant banks." A Nottingham developer reported the outcome of one sealed-bid auction involving 20 acres of building land: the property had gone to the bidder whose sealed letter simply read "£1250 an acre more than the highest bid made."

The immediate response of the Minister of Local Government and Development was to advise local authorities to use compulsory purchase powers where they thought hoarding was going on. At this the President of the National Housebuilders Federation wrote to *The Times* to announce that what was needed was "a surplus of land with planning permission in the hands of builders to prick the balloon of inflation." His wish was not long denied. In July the Standing Conference on London and South East Regional Planning published the results of a study which showed that planning authorities had already granted permission for enough new housebuilding to last the industry five years, even at record rates of output. In the South East alone there were current permissions for 320,000 dwellings. The builders themselves were the real bottleneck; with memories of bankruptcies during the credit squeeze still fresh in their minds they continued to be cautious. Despite the opprobrium heaped upon their heads at the time many were in due course to bless their own lack of enterprise.

No sooner had the "land hoarding" myth been exploded than a new London scandal erupted into the newspapers. Improvement grants, the subject of yet another Ministry of Housing publicity drive in April, were now shown to be engines of strife rather than a genuine alternative to comprehensive redevelopment. Figures produced by the Notting Hill Housing Trust showed that the grants, rather than going to small landlords, were being funnelled directly and indirectly into owner-occupation. Property companies in particular were gaining vacant possession of whole streets, turning houses into apartments for sale, and relying on improvement grants for up to two-thirds of their profits. Laurence Marks noted gloomily in *The Observer* ". . . the march of the carriage lamps and the mauve front doors across inner London is even more destructive of communities than redevelopment, where the local authority is at least responsible for rehousing the dispossessed." The grant programme had of course originated with the Labour government in the 1969 Housing Act, but it was aggressively promoted by the Conservatives during their period of office because the rising figures for grant approvals could be used to offset dismay over the poor performance of private builders during what was after all an unprecedented boom in demand.[1]

Notwithstanding the insight of a spokesman for the Nationwide Building Society who in June advised *The Evening Standard* that there were "signs of a slow-down," house prices rose in the third quarter of the year by a record 15%. In London the average price for a modern house was now over £11,000, more than a third higher than the national figure, and by the end of September that too was 42% higher than a year earlier. By a strange quirk of fate Labour controlled Newham borough council found itself caught in an inflationary trap.

Concerned at the low level of owner-occupation in Newham, as in other predominantly working-class London districts, the council had in 1969 launched a savings programme for 70 young couples then renting from the authority. At a cost of at least £3 a week these families were to save the deposits for houses then being built by the council so that, with the aid of local authority mortgages, they could move in on completion. With 57 houses occupied in this way the council enlarged the scheme and enrolled another 200 savers living in one-bedroom council flats. Unfortunately the construction cost of the dwellings earmarked for these tenants rose dramatically, and by the time they were finished at the end of 1972 the sale price without profit was so high that the saved deposits were inadequate to secure loans. In desperation a deputation from the council led by Mr Reginald Prentice went to the new Minister of Housing Mr Paul Channon with a request that the houses should be sold at discounts of up to £2000 so that the designated owners could in fact take possession.

By the end of 1972 a further 8% had been added to average prices, which now stood at just under £9000 for new houses. The societies themselves had advanced an unprecedented £3620

---

[1]In the three full years of the Conservative administration improvement grant approvals steadily increased, from 197,000 in 1971 to 319,169 in 1972 and then to a record 360,954 in 1973. In 1974 they fell to 231,918 and in 1975 to 126,888. The total cost of all improvement grants approved was £73,474,000 in 1971, £189,485,000 in 1972, £271,674,000 in 1973 and £263,311,000 in 1974. Nearly half the 360,954 grants approved in 1973 went to owner-occupiers. *Housing and Construction Statistics No 20*, 1976.

million in mortgages to a record 681,000 borrowers, with the former figure 85% up on the sum advanced only two years before. On paper net receipts were still rising with £1801 million added to assets in 1972, an increase smaller than 1971 over 1970 but still nearly 6% higher than the sum which had fuelled the start of the legendary boom: but unfortunately inflation was now an important factor and the net increase in real terms was zero. Even with the lending rate again raised to 8½% the societies would have to do £4000 million in new mortgage business in 1973 just to stay in the same place.

In the first three months of the new year the increase in house prices halved to 4%. This at first was hailed as good news, but there was clear evidence that the earning capacity of first-time borrowers had been outstripped by the previous year's price increases[1] and demand itself was faltering for the first time since 1970. In April the societies suddenly increased their mortgage interest rate to 9½%, even though their net inflow of funds remained high (as late as August seasonally adjusted figures still indicated a 7% increase over the whole year) and their outstanding commitments had fallen from the record £922 million of December 1972. In the same month the government, in an extraordinary move, lent the movement £15 million on condition that the mortgage interest rate did not rise to 10% within three months.

These blows, falling one after another, sent ripples of dismay through 4 million current mortgage holders as well as the count-less potential house buyers whose will-to-purchase had been whipped up to near hysteria by the events of the past eighteen months. Alas there was worse to come, and as the summer approached the true dimensions of the impending disaster became apparent. Underlying everything was the falling level of

---

[1]In 1963 the average borrower taking out an average building society advance of £2,148 had an income of £1,220 and was thus committed to paying 14% of his gross income for his mortgage. Ten years later, with the mortgage interest rate 4% higher at 10%, his repayments on a £5,500 average advance amounted to 24% of his gross income. Building society lending rules draw the line at advances larger than three times gross income, or annual repayments larger than 25% of net income. Thus by the autumn of 1973 the average building society borrower was on the very margin of creditworthiness: the gazumping boom had taken average house prices out of reach of average incomes. Figures: Graham Searjeant, *The Sunday Times* 2nd September 1973.

industrial production, poor export performance and widespread overseas borrowing which had accompanied the booming property market of the "dash for growth." As a consequence the pound had begun to falter on the international money market and, in order to prevent a massive flight of capital, London interest rates were forced to rise. At this point the elaborate measures taken in 1970 and 1971 to ensure that lending was controlled by the cost of borrowing, and not by fixed ceilings, cranked into action like a servo motor under automatic control. Before the horrified gaze of the Conservative government the interest paid on bank deposits levered itself off the 1971 floor of $2\frac{1}{2}\%$ and began to drive towards the building society rate, pushing all competitors ahead of it as though it were a bulldozer.[1] Under this remorseless pressure the societies embarked on a journey into inflation which was only to end three years later when the mortgage interest rate peaked at a record $12\frac{1}{4}\%$.

During the early summer of 1973 the Bank of England, alarmed at the turn events had taken, requested the clearing banks to hold their deposit rate at $9\frac{1}{2}\%$, just below the building societies investment rate of 9.64%. But the margin proved too narrow and in August the decision was taken to raise the societies' mortgage rate to 10%. The breaking of this psychological barrier unleashed a flood of criticism of the societies, the Conservative government and its entire economic policy. *The Daily Mirror* headlined its front page "Sorry young lovers" and quoted a "heartbroken" bride-to-be, robbed of the house she and her fiancé had saved for, "They can raise their percentages all they like, but they will never kill our dreams." Mr Reginald Freeson, who as housing minister in a later Labour government was to preside over an interest rate 2% higher, announced that the Conservatives were entirely responsible for dashing the hopes of so many young people.

In fact the crucial steps had already been taken by the time the increase was announced. The Bank of England had begun reducing

[1]The revision of the Bank of England arrangements for regulating lending, which came into effect in October 1971, replaced the old Bank Rate with a Minimum Lending Rate (MLR) with no fixed relationship to bank deposit rates. Provision was made at the time for regulation of bank deposit rates should the building societies be endangered. The bulldozer effect was to push building society mortgage interest rates up to $12\frac{1}{4}\%$ in 1976 despite regulation of some competitive interest rates.

the liquidity of the banking system by calling in special deposits in July, and the fact that house prices only rose by 3% in the third quarter of the year (the lowest rate of increase since 1969) was destined to have no effect on interest rates. In the final quarter of 1973 the rate of increase in house prices sank to less than half of 1%, but the mortgage interest rate rose again to 11% under the remorseless pressure of world-wide inflation and the necessity for high domestic interest rates to retain foreign holdings of sterling. Despite remarkable results for the year as a whole the building society movement was not sanguine about the future: in 1973 £3540 million had been advanced on mortgage (only 3% less than in 1972) to 554,000 borrowers (20% less than in 1972), but net receipts were down 16% to £1512 million, which was a serious matter against a background of retail price inflation approaching 10%. Sir Hubert Newton of the Leek and Westbourne Society set the tone at the end of August when he predicted 14% mortgages before long.[1]

With matters going badly astray in so many directions it would hardly have been surprising had the guilty expansionists linked arms in an effort to ward off approaching nemesis; and this indeed was what occurred. The modest government loan, which had temporarily stayed the arrival of the 10% mortgage rate, brought government and building societies closer together than at any time since the war. In October a Memorandum of Agreement was signed between them which established a number of joint objec-

[1]There was no immediate relationship between the rate of increase of house prices during the gazumping boom and the rate of increase in retail prices, which peaked much later. As the following table shows, the impact of the energy crisis was felt two years after the highest rate of house price increases.

End of Year	Retail Price Index (1970 = 100) and percentage Increase		Average New House Prices and percentage Increase	
1970	100	6.4%	£5,020	3.1%
1971	109.4	9.4%	£6,074	20.9%
1972	117.2	7.1%	£8,935	47.0%
1973	128.0	9.2%	£9,989	11.0%
1974	148.5	16.1%	£10,542	5.5%
1975	184.4	24.2%	£11,991	13.0%
1976	215.0	16.5%	£12,660	5.5%

Sources: Retail Price Index *Economic Trends* September 1977.
House prices: Nationwide Building Society to 1974. Published Department of the Environment figures thereafter.

tives: the continued support of owner-occupation; maintenance of a flow of mortgage funds sufficient for the construction industry to maintain a high and stable level of new housebuilding; the stabilisation of house prices, and the maintenance of choice for all purchasers.

To these somewhat nebulous ambitions the Memorandum added a rather more specific duty. Henceforth the Building Societies Association was to encourage a system of mortgage rationing when the supply of funds was low. A hierarchy was devised in which (assuming that all applicants were creditworthy) the first choice would be a purchaser with no previous mortgage history; the second any purchaser of a new dwelling; the third a second-time purchaser with compelling reasons for moving from his existing home; the fourth a second-time purchaser whose mortgage transaction would facilitate another transaction involving one of the preceding three choices; the fifth any other second-time purchaser, and finally a housing society or similar body related to the Housing Corporation.

Unfortunately the signatories of the Memorandum had both almost reached the end of their tether. Despite the action of the Bank of England in restraining competitive bank deposit rates, and despite the second increase in the mortgage interest rate to 11% in September, building society net receipts were still falling. In the first quarter of 1974 the movement recorded a net *outflow* of £21 million, an alarming sign, especially when coupled with the decline in mortgate repayments during 1973 which had resulted from a large number of hard-pressed borrowers failing to increase their payments in response to the rise in interest rates. This proved to be the last act in the gazumping drama, for the Conservative government itself fell in February. Mounting inflation combined with a legendary intransigence in Labour relations had made it extremely unpopular in Trades Union circles; an ill-timed Middle East war which led to a temporary oil embargo and a determined miners' strike created chaos in industry. The government's response was to declare a three-day working week and call a general election. By a supreme irony house prices were absolutely motionless (a thing which had not happened since the late 1950s) at the moment of Conservative eclipse. But on 28th February the Party suffered a serious defeat, losing 33 seats and over a million votes. The great gazumping boom was over.

8 The Turning Point

"Would £1500 be a help? Or £4000 or £5000? Or any other nice round figure in between? If you are a homeowner or buying your home on mortgage (sorry, no tenants), it's surprisingly simple for us to arrange a substantial secured loan. Thousands of home-owning clients in all parts of Britain have found our service quick and dependable. The terms are reasonable and have not changed. Even more important, perhaps, you will find that our attitudes are friendly. So why not fill in the form below now and drop it in the postbox. If you qualify, you will receive your cheque quickly."

John Ferguson, Financings
(Guarantees) Limited advertisement, June 1976

The return of a Labour government coincided with the first unmistakable signs that the crisis in the housing market might be accompanied by a catastrophe in the property business as a whole. In December 1973 London and County Securities, a fringe bank heavily involved in property, crashed with a loss of £50 million. Then in January 1974 a large City of London office block, valued in 1973 at £35 million, failed to find a buyer at only £20 million. Clearly it was worth less than its owners believed and, if that was so, what was the real value of all the other real estate into which not only speculators but banks, insurance companies and pension funds had poured investment over the last few years? In 1973 the Conservative government, embarrassed by massive profits in the property sector, had frozen business rents. Now it became clear that the boom had been accompanied by the abuses and mis-judgements which only rapidly rising values cover up. Property companies had indulged heavily in deficit financing (whereby the income from the property they purchased fell far short of the interest payable on the money they had borrowed to buy it) on the assumption that increases in value would go on. With the un-critical, even naive, aid of clearing banks, merchant banks, secondary banks and foreign banks (all of whom frequently advanced 100% of valuations) massive purchases had been made whose fundamental unsoundness now required at least £300 million in cash support if foreclosures were not to bankrupt major companies, create unemployment and damage still further the prestige of London as a financial centre. This last factor counted for much, even with a Labour government which at last had the hated property developers in its power, and in the event contributed to the underwriting of the property sector which limited the extent of the disaster. Nation Life property bonds collapsed in the summer, followed by Triumph Investment Trust in November, but most survived as a result of the decontrol of business rents which the Labour government permitted in February 1975. The Labour Party determined to exact a price for this grudging support, but in the spring of 1974 there were more urgent issues confronting it.

At the 1973 Party Conference, before their return to power, the socialists had committed themselves to a seven-point housing programme designed to redress the wrongs of the gazumping era whilst not unduly alarming the electorally important owner-occupiers. The most novel feature was a return to the unsuccessful 1955 policy of municipalisation, the purchase of private dwellings by local authorities in order to "eliminate private landlordism once and for all." Another long standing measure, the nationalisation of development land, was proposed as a means of controlling house prices. It was claimed that it would wipe out "speculators" and "land hoarders" whilst leaving the freehold of the owner-occupier intact. Labour's goodwill towards home owners was to be proved by an increased supply of 100% mortgages and universal extension of the option mortgage scheme, both of which measures were designed to help the first-time buyer. With the pill of land nationalisation buried in the sugar of house-price controls, the Party also felt free to promise increased council house building as well. Resolutions demanding the restriction of improvement grants so as to keep them out of the hands of the owners of second homes, the nationalisation of land belonging to the Royal Family and others whose ancestors had "stolen it from the people" were proposed, applauded and not adopted.

The inconclusive outcome of the February 1974 general election, from which Labour emerged with only the tiniest of parliamentary majorities, offered the Party an unique opportunity to assume responsibility for the housing and property problem, but little power to do anything about it. Within weeks the new government was involved in distasteful rescue operations in the commercial property sector as well as urgent talks with the building societies, who were intent on raising the mortgage interest rate to 13% in order to revive investment. If the ill-fated Conservative government had loaned the societies money in order to delay the arrival of the 10% rate, their successors would hardly endear themselves to the voters by permitting it to rise 3% higher still at a time when a second general election was almost inevitable. Consequently the government agreed to make £500 million in short-term credits available to prevent the increase—a sum considerably larger than that mooted for the salvation of the entire commercial property sector and the troubled secondary banks which had involved themselves with it.

The Labour government clearly thought it sufficient in a time of economic crisis to spare the existing privileges of the owner-occupiers while concentrating their attention on the growing problem of inflation. As early as January 1974 the editor of the London financial newspaper *City Press* had pointed out that a young man or woman earning £2000 a year at the age of twenty-one would require £200,000 at retiring age in order to maintain their standard of living. The Conservative Party took a different view. Recovering quickly from the shock of their electoral defeat they published an election manifesto in August intended to restore their fortunes should the Labour Party endeavour to improve its position by holding another poll in the autumn. In return for voting Conservative Mrs Margaret Thatcher, the new shadow minister of the environment, offered an "unshakeable pledge" that the mortgage interest rate would be cut to 9½% by Christmas. She also offered "Home Savings Grants" of one pound for every two pounds saved by would-be home owners; a law to permit all local authority tenants of three years standing to buy their homes at one third less than market price and, most radical of all, the progressive abolition of the domestic local authority rate over a period of five years.

Since at the time the building societies were drawing on the Labour government's £500 million loan, there is some justification for the view that the socialists had already raised the betting on the owner-occupier vote. Nonetheless the Conservative plan, denounced by the Labour Minister of the Environment Mr Anthony Crosland as "a pack of lies", was a clear indication that the Party had decided to devote every available resource to the battle for the hearts and minds of the home owners in the coming election. Notwithstanding Labour criticism the Thatcher plan was an ingenious measure. The $9\frac{1}{2}\%$ mortgage rate was to be paid for by a reduction of about £200 million a year in the composite rate of tax paid by the societies on behalf of their investors: accelerated council house sales would restore local authority housing revenue accounts to credit; and the "Home Savings Grants" would ensure the allegiance not only cf those who already owned their own homes, but of those many thousands imbued with a desperate desire to do so. Only the abolition of the domestic rate seemed a perverse idea, robbing the local authorities of a primary source of income which would simply have to be made good by some other form of taxation. Politically all four elements of the plan had a direct appeal to the crucial voters: high mortgage interest rates, recent increases in the local authority rate coupled with an emergency rates levy, and the increasingly difficult task of saving for a home that was growing more expensive every day, were all directly attacked—while the cost of the whole programme was to be diffused amongst all taxpayers so that the burden on the owner occupiers themselves would be eased yet again.

From the alarm generated in the Labour government and the extensive discussion provoked among political commentators it is clear that many expected the Conservative bid for the home owners' vote to swing the coming election back to them; and in the sense of once again depriving Labour of an overall majority it almost did.[1] But the Thatcher plan had ignored other issues of equal concern to owner-occupiers and aspirants to that status. 1974 was the year in which, after missing a full generation, the

---

[1]Because the Thatcher plan failed to win the October 1974 election for the Conservatives, the alarm which it generated at the time has been forgotten. Writing in *The Sunday Times* (22nd September 1974) John Barry noted "Conservative leaders, convinced that housing lost them the February election, are also aware that this is their most promising issue. Private opinion polls, taken in the 47 critical seats where they are concentrating their resources, have persuaded party managers that there is nothing better to hammer home."

term unemployment came again to mean something terrifyingly irrevocable: the year in which a British government minister rode humbly in a Mini behind the Cadillac of a Saudi Arabian Sheikh: the year in which desperate unilateral oil deals almost sundered the painfully united countries of the European Common Market: the year in which British citizens bought South African Kruger-rands to the value of £9 million every week. The Conservative record on industrial relations, the miners' strike and the three day week, had disturbed even their most loyal supporters: of what use was a new mortgage and a house doubling in value every five years if the country was in uproar? The general election held on 10th October produced a poll 6% lower than in February, and the Conservative share of the vote dropped by a further 2%; sufficient to rob them of another 20 seats in the House of Commons.

If the year 1974 marked something of a watershed in British politics, with its two inconclusive elections and the flood of critical economic issues consequent upon the world recession caused by the massive increase in oil prices, it also marked universal political and economic acceptance of the new importance of the home owners in the national economy. The great advance of the gazumping years, although halted at the very moment of conquest by the failure of the Thatcher plan in the October general election, was not turned back. Instead the home owners settled down to consolidate their vast new territories in the popular imagination and the national balance sheet. True, they had not moved forward into the wonderland of privilege offered them by the Conservative Party, but neither had they fallen back into the low priority traditionally assigned to them in the socialist scheme of things. Like climbers on some economic Everest the owner-occupiers stood then where they stand now, within a few hundred feet of the summit, conscious that the short remaining distance might cheat them of the ultimate prize.

This uncertainty was inevitable, for it was not only a 40-year tradition of single party rule that was ended by the polls of 1974, but the much longer separation of powers which permitted the building societies to act independently of government, and governments to plan housing programmes without consultation with the building societies. The 1973 Memorandum of Agreement between the Conservative government and the Building Societies Association had led to the creation of a Joint Advisory Commttee on Building Society Mortgage Finance, and this committee in turn had set up a technical sub-committee to consider forecasts and analyses of the private housing market. The Labour government, confirmed in power though still with a wafer-thin majority, took over these consultative arrangements and in April 1975 reached a further agreement under which the supply of mortgage money made available by the building societies was henceforth to be regulated in order to prevent large fluctuations such as the surge which contributed to the house price explosion of 1972. This measure of restraint, although lacking the force of legislation, marked a minor concession by the building societies in return for which they obtained the promise of cooperation from the Labour government on a wide variety of issues, including the enlargement of permissible construction loans to builders, previously strictly controlled. In fact it appeared by the beginning of 1975 that the only request of the societies that the government had refused to grant was a thinly disguised version of the "Home Savings Grants" promised by the Conservatives, turned down on the grounds that the cost to the exchequer would be too great.

The support for the private property sector, the £500 million loan to the building societies, and the promise to make further loans should the movement experience difficulties in attracting sufficient investment (which was combined with a reciprocal promise to allow the societies to invest with the government at $10\frac{1}{2}\%$ interest should restrictions on mortgage advances by the Joint Advisory Committee create an embarrassment of funds), marked a new phase in the relationship of the building societies with the Labour Party. No doubt in part it was an inevitable result of the mounting external economic crisis which compelled the Labour government to impose increasing restrictions on public expenditure in an effort (the third in 30 years) to reverse an accumulating balance of payments deficit; but in part also it came from a belated recognition of the enormous power of the building societies themselves, leaning as it did upon the manifest desire of many millions of voters to own their own homes. The complicity with the owner-occupiers which was politically required of the second 1974 Labour government, attained an even greater importance when a succession of by-election losses drove them into a status of government-by-alliance which they had not experienced since the Great Depression. The public spending cuts forced on them by the terms of necessary external loans hit first the supply of local authority mortgages, and later the subsidies to local government upon which both council house building plans and the municipalisation of the last strongholds of the private landlords were founded. The final throw, which was a further exploration of the possibility of using "prefabs", converted double garage units, caravans and mobile homes, met with united opposition from every section of the housebuilding industry. With 50,000 unsold houses in England and Wales, and 200,000 either under construction or with planning permission, the builders already faced mounting unemployment and bankruptcies rising steeply to the level of the years before the gazumping boom. The local authorities reacted coldly to a Ministry circular issued in March 1975 which forbade the construction of garages on new council estates and suggested the abandonment of official space standards in order to permit the purchase of speculatively built private houses and the negotiation of contracts with private builders and developers. When in May the local authority mortgage allocation was cut by £100 million, the disparity between the collapsing public housing effort and the renewed strength of the building societies was made painfully evident. The sum, which virtually took the local authorities out of the private housing market, represented only an average week's lending to the societies. By July the building societies, notwithstanding the 11% interest rate, were approving 60,000 home loans a month—a number equivalent to the level of lending at the height of the gazumping boom in 1972. Under these terms, their own housing plans in ruins, the Labour government had no alternative but to make peace with the "mere moneylenders" of thirty years before. The housing effort of the state, which had grown from virtual non-existence before the Great War to the support of five million families, had reached a condition of paralysis; while the owner occupiers—equally insignificant before 1914—stood nine million strong, backed by the enormous economic power of the building societies, in virtual mastery of the government.

Between 1970 and 1973, although the market value of all privately owned dwellings in England and Wales cannot be precisely determined, all authorities agree that it doubled. According to a formula derived from the average of rateable values and market prices for mortgageable houses it increased from about

£32,000 million in 1970 to £67,000 million by the end of 1973. During the same period gross domestic capital formation (gross investment) increased by only 8%, from £9453 million to £10,253 million.[1] In 1973 the estimated market value of the nine million owner-occupied dwellings in England and Wales (£67,000 million) was greater than the value at current replacement cost of all the buildings, vehicles, ships, aircraft, plant and works belonging to industrial and commercial companies in the United Kingdom. In 1974, a year in which building society advances were down by 19% on the record set in 1972 and the number of loans on houses had dropped by nearly 40%, the 6% increase in the value of the average owner-occupied house meant a gross increase in value of over £4000 million—a sum approximately equal to the cost of developing all known oil reserves in the North Sea from 1975 to 1980, or four times the development costs of Concorde.

An even more compelling indication of the new economic importance of home ownership as a medium of investment can be gained by comparing real net manufacturing investment with net investment in building societies. In 1970 the former stood at £1040 million and the latter at £1213 million: by 1974 manufacturing investment had fallen to £791 million and building society receipts had also fallen, but only to £1165 million. In 1976, when recovery from the 1974 investment crisis was complete, manufacturing investment amounted to only £365 million while the net receipts of the building society movement totalled

---

[1] The Central Statistical Office publication *National Income and Expenditure 1966-76* lists the value of the net capital stock at current replacement cost of all dwellings in the United Kingdom as £20,200 million in 1970 and £38,200 million in 1973. These estimates are based on rateable values which are lower than market values. By averaging the owner-occupier component of these figures with the product of average mortgageable house prices for the same two years (*Housing and Construction Statistics* No 20) the approximations used in the text were reached. The remainder of the figures used in this paragraph were obtained as follows. Gross domestic capital formation, *National Income and Expenditure*. Fixed assets of commercial and industrial companies, *National Income and Expenditure*. North Sea oil development cost estimate, *The Sunday Times Business News* 9th February 1975. Concorde development cost assumed to be around £1,000 million.

£2448 million,[1] somewhat lower than the £3191 million received in 1975, but still double the 1974 figure.

This spectacular increase in building society investment, and the corresponding decline in support for manufacturing industry, were both results of the proven performance of owner-occupied—as opposed to commercial—property during the crisis which coincided with the collapse of the gazumping boom and the world recession. At the time of the second general election of 1974 average industrial shares had lost 80% of their 1968 value and prices on the London stock exchange stood at the level of June 1940 when a German invasion appeared to be only weeks away. Between 1970 and 1974 nine major stock exchange firms crashed with combined losses in excess of £6 million; each collapse involved checking through six or seven tons of paper and comprised enough work to keep the Official Assignee's office employed for up to three years.

Against such a background the performance of private housing looked little short of miraculous. While other investments collapsed like houses of cards real houses not only kept pace with inflation but actually outstripped it. Between 1970 and 1974 the retail price index[2] rose from 100 to 215 while the average price for new, mortgage-approved dwellings climbed from 100 to 259. Investors rapidly drew the appropriate conclusions and the resultant flood of money into the building societies was dramatic. From the net outflow recorded in the first quarter of 1974 deposits rose steadily until in January 1975 net receipts of £293 million bettered the previous all-time record of £225 million received in July 1973. During the second quarter of 1975 the societies received nearly £1000 million in net receipts, but even this figure remained unbeaten only until the first quarter of 1976 when £1043 was deposited—a figure larger than the total assets of the building

[1]Real net manufacturing investment at current replacement cost for 1970, 1974 and 1976, Walter Eltis, *The Sunday Times* 4th December 1977. Building society net receipts for 1970, 1974 and 1976, *Facts and Figures No 11 July 1977*, published by the Building Societies Association.
[2]Retail price index *Economic Trends* September 1977. Index for average price of mortgage-approved dwellings *Housing and Construction Statistics No 20*. The building society investment figures used in the remainder of this paragraph are taken from *Facts and Figures (op cit)*.

society movement in 1950. Altogether the savings held by the building societies movement increased by £7700 million from the end of 1974 to the end of 1976, more money than it had attracted in the first sixty years of the 20th century.

This staggering increase in economic power transformed the nature of the building societies. From their historic role as a relatively low-yield repository for the modest savings of thrifty citizens they had grown first into major financial institutions under the control of professional managers, and now into a cartel holding the largest cash investment in the country. Although the decision taken by the Building Societies Association in 1974 to refer to the movement henceforth as an *industry* was later reversed, the expansion from assets of £11,000 million in 1970 to £30,000 million in 1977 is better understood as a change in economic function than as a simple process of growth. The magnitude of this change can be seen in many ways, perhaps most visibly in the entirely new pattern of advertising employed by the societies.

Since the gazumping boom it is assumed that demand exists for whatever sums can be made available for mortgages, and this once prominent aspect of building society publicity has thus disappeared. Instead overwhelming emphasis is laid upon investment plans of various kinds, with references to houses limited to the figurative as in the archetypal Bradford and Bingley society poster of 1977 in which one top-hatted investor observes to another "A safe home, Mr Bradford". To which his companion replies "For your money, Mr Bingley." In the same way the Abbey National society, which since its creation by merger during the Second World War has built its advertising around the well known picture of a couple striding arm in arm into the future under an umbrella fashioned from the roof of a house, now relegates this poignant image to diminutive size and encloses it within a raised thumb: a symbol of the "Abbey habit" of saving whose terms are spelled out by means of large percentage figures occupying the display space. Moving in the same direction the Woolwich now makes great play of the resemblance of the double "o" in its name to a percentage symbol, while Nationwide (which modestly describes itself as "The building society of a lifetime") has adopted an ingenious "£" whose tail angles back into a diagrammatic roof, and the Chelsea society has converted the middle "l" of its name into an "£" with a circumflex above it to denote growth.

A second indication of change in the function of the building societies can be seen in the increasing importance which is attached to medium and long-term investment as opposed to the traditional dependence on short term deposits made by small savers. This change, which can be detected in the increasing proportion of society income attributable to interest credited,[1] marks the abandonment of one of the cardinal points of building society policy since the earliest days of the movement. From the time of the great building society failures at the end of the 19th century, heavy emphasis had always been laid upon the instant accessibility of funds deposited with the movement; a measure essential when the target investor was an individual of limited means. In recent years this pattern has altered with the development of a wide range of investment plans designed to attract larger sums of money committed for three, five or ten years. To aid this process limits on the size of individual share accounts have been progressively eased and bypassed.

The third and most important aspect of change within the building societies has been their adjustment to the emergence of home ownership itself as a form of investment, a development which will be dealt with at some length in the following chapter, but which owes its origins to the new demographic and political parameters of home ownership established since the gazumping boom, which differ considerably from those in effect over the preceding twenty years.

Between the fall of the 1951 Labour government and the beginning of dramatic house price inflation in 1971, the proportion of public and private housing built in England and Wales was roughly equal, so that in terms of new construction each sector was increasing in size at about the same rate. Out of the 12.4 million dwellings recorded by the 1951 census, approximately 4.5 million were owner-occupied. Twenty years later this

---

[1] The percentage of interest credited in the composite figure for net receipts *and* interest credited published by the Building Societies Association (*Facts and Figures* Nos 8 and 11) shows a significant increase since 1974. The average from end 1970 to end 1973 was interest 21 %, capital 79 %. The average for end 1973 to end 1976 was interest 31 %, capital 69 %.

number had increased to 8.8 million out of 17 million. Over the same two decades the number of public sector dwellings (local authorities and new towns) increased from 1.8 million to 4.9 million. The disparity in the growth of the two sectors was caused by the absorption of over one million dwellings from the private rental sector into owner-occupation, and not by any inequity in rates of new construction.

Until the introduction of municipalisation in 1974 (it was first proposed in the 1950s while Labour was in opposition) the only means open to the socialists to combat this "unfair" advantage enjoyed by the private sector was the extensive demolition of poor-quality privately rented housing in order to prevent it from eventually falling into the hands of owner-occupiers. In this sense the growing opposition to comprehensive redevelopment on social and economic grounds, which came to the foreground in the 1960s, would have posed a serious indirect threat to the growth of local authority housing in urban areas had not the Labour government which took office in 1966 introduced the improvement grant system, whose chief beneficiaries were intended to be the local authorities themselves.

This attempted restoration of a balance in owner-occupier and local authority access to the disintegrating private rental sector was rudely shattered by the coming of the Conservative government in 1970. By stressing the availability of improvement grants for the modernisation and sale of privately rented urban housing, and threatening rent increases and sales within the public sector itself, the Conservatives created a short breakthrough for the owner-occupiers which ensured that the growth in home ownership between 1971 and 1974 exceeded the average established in the preceding twenty years. It was probably the last occasion on which sales from the private rental sector played a significant part in the growth of home ownership. As *The Building Societies' Gazette*[1] noted in September 1976:

"Between 1967 and 1974 the number of owner occupied houses increased by an average of 247,000 a year but private sector completions averaged only 186,000 a year. An additional 20,000

[1] Mark Boléat, "Home ownership may not reach 60% this decade." *The Building Societies' Gazette* September 1976.

houses a year entered the owner occupied sector through council sales but far out-weighing this were the 83,000 a year demolitions, the vast majority of which were in the private sector. The best estimate is that some 70,000 houses a year have been transferred from the private rented to the owner occupied sector—a rate that clearly cannot continue given that many houses left in the private rented sector are not suitable for owner occupation."

The importance of the forthcoming exhaustion of the private rental sector cannot be over emphasised. It represents a change in the circumstances surrounding the growth of home ownership of an order not experienced since the deliberate suppression of private sector construction by the Labour government of 1945. During the six post-war years reliance upon sales out of rental was complete: a situation which will soon be entirely reversed, for current projections anticipate an almost total reliance on new construction which, in relation to recent demographic projections, is equivalent to predicting the end of the battle of the tenures at last. Unfortunately such calculations do not take into account the real political and economic power which now underlies demand for home ownership. Neither do they recognise the major changes which the new economic function of the building societies have made possible in the owner-occupier market. Most important of all they show no understanding of the enormous difference in value between owner-occupation and other forms of tenure in a consumer society.

9 The Owner Speculators

"I'm not the least interested in houses as such and I'd be quite happy living in a tent, but I'm excited by the financial possibilities of houses. I regard it as a form of earning because I don't work."

"We're having the kitchen and breakfast room bashed down to make an absolutely super, incredibly flash kitchen, and we're doing the same with the bathrooms and loos. It will cost about £3000, and as soon as it's done it will go on the market."

Voices from the Middle Class
Deverson and Lindsay 1975

If there is one constant in the history of home ownership it is the all but accidental nature of its growth. From the earliest times it has been the product of conflicting economic and political forces, virtually none of which had as their principal object the enlargement of owner-occupation. Indeed, as even the short account contained in this book makes clear, so instrumental has the pursuit of home ownership been that only recently was it identified as a unitary phenomenon. Not until 1961 was the national census (which has in its long history been used to determine such matters as the number of blind, deaf and dumb persons, and the number speaking Gaelic) modified so as to show the tenure of households, and all estimates of the extent of home ownership before that date are based upon deductions from information gathered for other purposes.

From medieval times the pursuit of freehold tenure was synonymous with the attainment of full political rights, a factor which was of overwhelming importance as late as the mid 19th-century, when it contributed to the growth of the building societies, and which did not entirely disappear until the Reform Act of 1884. From that date until the outbreak of the Great War the purchase of a house or houses was as often the prelude to a career as a landlord as it was to the achievement of home ownership in its own right. Even after the introduction of rent control in 1915 the first sustained period of growth of home ownership which ended in 1939 had more the character of an effect than a cause. Between the wars householders bought houses either because no comparable dwellings were available for rent, or because landlords offered at bargain prices assets which had been transformed into liabilities by events beyond their control. This process continued throughout the Second World War and the subsequent Labour administration, a period which in all other respects presented a hostile climate to any kind of new construction in the private sector.

During the 1950s, when for the first time a sizeable market in owner-occupied dwellings built without thought of rental did come into existence, the matter was still not resolved politically. The 1957 Rent Act and its socialist rejoinder of 1965 were both measures taken for and against landlordism at a time when home ownership, almost unnoticed, was fast becoming the most important form of tenure. Political recognition of this fact brought two major changes: it ended argument over whether the private rental sector could or should be revived, and it began the process of competition between the two major parties for the owner-occupier's vote. In this new battle the case for owner-occupation was unanswerable in so far as neither party dared openly oppose it, but this in turn placed the Labour Party at a disadvantage. Owing to the immense political importance of the five million households tenanting publicly owned housing (virtually all of whom were assumed to vote socialist) the Labour Party could not afford to allow this form of tenure to degenerate into a second reservoir of potentially saleable dwellings. Consequently it maintained a rate of public sector construction equal to, if not greater than, that operating in the private sector even as it offered qualified aid to would-be home owners through local authority mortgages and the option mortgage scheme.

The acute economic crisis of the 1970s placed this arrangement in jeopardy for two reasons. First because the sums available for new public sector construction and the rents received from council housing both declined, and second because home ownership increasingly demonstrated real economic advantages as far as the householder was concerned. The latter process was, as we have seen, deliberately abetted by the policies of the Conservative Party both in power and in opposition and, for fear of losing owner-occupier votes, could not be effectively restrained by the socialists.[1]

Here again the instrumentality of home ownership reveals itself, albeit in a modified form, for the dominant system of tenure of our time has never truly lost the contingency of its early years. Treated simply as a form of tenure, owner-occupation has no substantive advantages or disadvantages over rental; particularly when (as now) mortgage payments are accepted as a more or less continuous expenditure, no sooner paid off on one dwelling than assumed again on another. It is only when its economic, social and political implications are spelled out in the context of a consumer society that the real differences emerge, for in a consumer society tenure achieves its greatest importance in so far as it maximises or minimises consumption. And it is here that home ownership reveals unassailable advantages which assure its primacy.

Of the economic, social and political implications of owner-occupation the first is overwhelmingly the most important since it is the generator of the other two. If property in the economic sense can be defined as the exclusive use of wealth, then home ownership has become in a variety of complementary ways a creator of wealth in the form of purchasing power. In the sense that social and political advantages can never be divorced from wealth, this has probably always been true; but to the extent that political independence and social standing are now mass phenomena it is now more true than ever. The evolution of consumer societies in which the bulk of the population constitutes the largest market for goods and services has transformed the meaning of home ownership and re-ordered the benefits which flow from it. Today a political majority of the population of Britain enjoys advantages which once belonged to a tiny minority, and the advantages themselves have changed from an assembly of privi-

---

[1]In addition to international pressures which compelled public spending cuts, the Labour government was confronted with a situation in which the government subsidy component of the housing revenue account was rapidly overtaking the contribution made by rents. In 1975–76 and 1976–77 the total government subsidy exceeded £900 million while rents peaked £50 million lower, a complete reversal of the situation which had existed before 1974.

leges into a supply of products. It is this change which has made purchasing power more important than status, and the wealth-producing power of home ownership more important than home ownership itself.

The means by which home owners derive wealth from their dwellings developed over a number of years but were thrown into sharp relief by the events of the 1971–73 gazumping boom; at which time they became so universally obvious that the nature of demand for owner-occupied housing underwent a massive change as a result. At the most elementary level the boom demonstrated, as we have seen, that home ownership could represent an effective hedge against inflation, and consequently talk of house purchase as a good investment ceased to be figurative or long-term and became instead a matter of immediate importance. The logic of which change can be clearly seen by representing the increases in the value of housing estimated in the last chapter in terms of the gains of individual householders.

Between the end of 1970 and the end of 1973 the average price of new dwellings on which mortgages were made in England and Wales rose from £5020 to £10,690, a gross increase of £5670 or 112%. Since only just over half a million new houses were completed during this period, this figure cannot be held to apply to all of the nine million owner-occupied houses in existence in 1973, but the period began with a market in which new houses were worth more than existing houses and ended with existing houses worth more than new houses, so the difference is probably not great. On the other hand the number of houses sold during the three years was only a small proportion of the entire owner-occupied stock, and not all that stock can be regarded as mortgageable. Thus the maximum figure for the increase in value (nine million multiplied by £5670) is clearly too high. On the other hand the figure produced by the Central Statistical Office, which shows an increase of £18,000 million for the same period[1] is equally obviously too low. Taking the median of the two suggests an increase in value of about £34,000 million, or £3700 per individual owner-occupier. Whilst it is clear that the increase in value would not have been universally distributed with this degree of egalitarianism, it is also clear that the sums involved,

---

[1]*National Income and Expenditure 1966–67 (op cit).*

even at the individual level, were considerable. £3700 is after all equivalent to three year's mortgage payment on a sum of at least £10,000.

No tenant in the country, public or private, enjoyed any such advantage during the years 1970 to 1973. Even if the estimated increase in wealth is reduced by correcting for inflation the balance of advantage is not changed. Furthermore such increases in value were not confined to the height of the gazumping boom. Between the end of 1973 and the end of 1974 house prices increased by only 6%, but this was sufficient to produce a gross increase in value of over £4000 million; a sum equivalent to a capital gain of £500 for every home owner in England and Wales. Even in 1977, a year which began with the building societies' mortgage interest rate standing at an unprecedented 12.25%, the average value of a mortgageable house rose by £1000 to £13,200 and made a profit of £20 a week for every owner-occupier. In effect every mortgage holder with a mortgage debt of less than £8000 has lived free since 1970 because of the annual increase in the value of his or her home. Indeed so great has been the effect of increases in the value of owner-occupied dwellings that the total value of homes as a proportion of gross personal wealth[1] rose from 19.1% in 1960 to 38.8% in 1974.

Annual average house price figures indicate that capital gains of this order have been growing in importance for nearly 20 years, although it is difficult to determine exactly what part they played in boosting demand for home ownership before the enormous gains of the gazumping period made them common knowledge. In the light of such tangible advantages it would seem to have been naive to ascribe the popularity of owner-occupation to "a deep call of human nature", even in 1965; while to attribute the frenzy of the early 1970s to a desire for creative freedom in the matter of decoration was—in view of the source of the statement—plainly evasive. There can be little doubt that motives other than financial advantage do play a role in the popular preference for purchase, but the evidence clearly suggests that it need only be a minor one, for the economic inducements are enormous.

Once it is established that home owners do benefit from rising

[1]The conclusion of a Labour Party Research Department pamphlet *Inequality in Britain Today*, published in June 1977.

house prices, it is logical to inquire whether they themselves play a part in pushing them up, a question which can best be answered by taking a closer look at what happens in the mortgage market, which is of course overwhelmingly dominated by the building societies.

According to 1971 census data there were in that year 8.86 million owner-occupied dwellings in England and Wales; a number corresponding to 52.1% of all dwellings. By the end of 1976, according to estimates made in the 1977 *Housing Policy Review*,[1] their number had increased to 9.97 million (55.1%), a net gain of 1.1 million dwellings. During the same period the building societies made 2.87 million loans on houses in England and Wales,[2] and received 2.2 million mortgage terminations; a net gain of 673,500 new mortgage holders. The difference between this net gain and the 1.1 million increase in owner-occupied dwellings is explained by the number of houses which were during the period either bought outright, bought with the aid of other financial institutions such as insurance companies, or were the object of redeemed mortgages, so that they were added to the stock of owner-occupier houses without at the same time increasing the number of dwellings currently mortgaged.

The curious factor here is that the building societies, who maintain a distinction between first-time mortgages and those granted to existing mortgage holders who sell one house in order to buy another, record that 1.47 million first time mortgages were started between 1971 and 1976—even though the total increase in home ownership during the period was somewhat less at 1.1 million. The key to this conflict is the velocity of sales within the owner-occupier market rather than in the rate of addition to the stock of owner-occupied dwellings. Since on the basis of the number of new houses completed it is clear that the building societies are responsible for about 80% of all new house financing, we can assume that they financed about 900,000 out of the 1.1

---

[1] *Housing Policy Review* Technical Volume 1, HMSO 1977, page 152, tables III.35 and III.36.
[2] All figures for building society mortgages in this and the following paragraph are based upon the Building Societies Association *Facts and Figures* (*op cit*) tables for the United Kingdom rounded down by 5 % so as to exclude Scotland and Northern Ireland.

million, even though this figure is lower than the number of first-time mortgages granted during the period. But this strongly suggests that the distinction between first-time borrowers and existing mortgage holders becomes meaningless over a five-year time span. The only way in which all these figures can be reconciled is by accepting that many first-time borrowers become "recycling" mortgagors so rapidly that the real gearing of mortgage supply—the engine that powers the growth of home ownership—is now dropping from two to one (the ratio suggested by building society figures) to three to one. So that it is now true to say that the bulk of building society business is with "recycled" mortgages.

This tendency is an important aspect of the change in the function of the building societies which was described in the last chapter, and its effect on building society operations can be clearly seen in Fig. 1 which shows the relative importance of

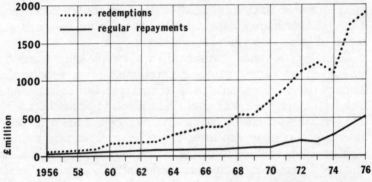

Fig. 1   The composition of mortgage repayments 1956–76. Reproduced from *Facts and Figures*, the quarterly bulletin of the Building Societies Association, issue number 10, April 1977.

mortgage redemptions and mortgage payments since 1956. While the graph makes clear the gradual increase in the importance of redemptions since a period of twenty years, it also shows the dramatic growth which has occurred since 1974. In 1976 no less than 80% of all mortgage payments made to the building societies took the form of redemptions (£1987 million out of £2487 million), with the net result that virtually none of the money repaid by existing borrowers was available for lending to first-time buyers.

It is of course true that not all redemptions are the result of owner-occupiers trading up in order to make capital gains out of rising house prices. The building societies themselves stress that emigration, divorce and death play a part. Nonetheless their own figures indicate[1] that between 80 and 90% of all redemptions are linked with new loans taken out.

The Building Societies Association holds the view that the cost of buying and selling houses and removing households is too high for trading up to be profitable, despite figures which make this conclusion hard to defend.[2] It has of course every interest in maintaining the somewhat temporary distinction between first-time borrowers and "recycling" mortgagors since this presents a more attractive picture of the owner-occupier market than the facts really warrant, but there can be little doubt that the societies sustain a growing element of what might be called owner-speculation, or house-trading motivated by the prospect of capital gain; a practice which substantially dates from the lessons learned during the gazumping boom and the change in the nature of the appeal of home ownership brought about by it.

The claim, repeatedly advanced, that capital gains made by trading up are merely paper or unrealisable profit because the home owner has to pay an equally inflated price for the next house he buys, ignores the extent to which he is able to plough his equity into his new purchase (by taking out a mortgage of the same value on a larger or more expensive house) or even to take a profit without selling at all by using the increasing value of his dwelling as a credit guarantee. Even more significantly such claims take no account of the manner in which increasing house values pay for the cost of mortgaging houses even if no such profit is taken.

In a resale-dominated owner-occupier market there are clearly no grounds for optimism in the matter of house prices. Not only is it in no-one's interest for house prices to stabilise or fall—except perhaps that of the would-be owner-occupier *before* he actually buys—but any such eventuality would clearly threaten the financial stability not only of the nine million households which

[1] The Building Societies Association *Facts and Figures* April 1977, page 18 Mortgage Repayments.
[2] *Housing Policy* Technical Volume 1 concludes that an average transaction cost for owner-occupier movers might be £500. Compared to the estimates of equity given above this clearly permits capital gains.

have come to depend to a greater or lesser extent on annual increases in capital wealth to finance part of their household consumption, but of the holders of 19 million building society share accounts whose enormous investment is secured upon the value of dwellings. Like the company car, the appreciating house has become an accepted part of the domestic economy of the suburban family and, because of the political importance of that family, it will be taken away by any government at its peril.

The new dependence of the owner-occupying household upon equity for part of its purchasing power is a phenomenon with important implications. Sales of consumer durables, frequently made on credit, are more often than not secured against freehold ownership: thus the manufacturers, importers and retailers of cars, freezers, washing machines, colour television sets, sound systems, furniture, garden accessories and so on in their turn rely on the appreciating value of houses to maintain demand for their products. Not only does home ownership now attract investment that might otherwise increase the efficiency of productive industry in competitive export markets, but the sums so invested are loaned against the security of dwellings whose increasing value actually contributes to imports through the creation of unearned purchasing power.[1] The seriousness with which this latter problem was viewed as recently as 1974 has since diminished under the emollient effect of North Sea oil revenues; but like other critical areas in the British economy it will not go away.

Once it is grasped that an increasing proportion of building society mortgage business concerns transactions which involve a sizeable capital gain, then the extent to which demand for economic opportunity underlies demand for home ownership becomes evident. And it is this underlying demand, the insistence upon a wider distribution of the only form of tenure with private wealth-creating capacity, which distinguishes the pursuit of home ownership in our own time from any previous historical manifestation of it.

Home ownership and the demand for home ownership on the part of those in other tenures constitutes a powerful political force today,

[1] Consider for example the economic implications of widespread use of home owners equity as collateral for the purchase of Japanese cars on credit.

but that force is itself a reflection of the enormous economic advantages of owner-occupation. For without the rising value of their dwellings, and the massive investment attracted by it, the home owners would be as impotent as were the equally numerous private landlords of an earlier time. It is because they are wealthy that the home owners are powerful; and because they are powerful they will exercise their political influence in order to protect their wealth.

Since the 19th century the growth of home ownership has brought housing full circle. When nine out of every ten dwellings in England and Wales were rented from private landlords, housing produced an income in the form of rent. Today, when more than half the dwellings in the same geographical area are owner-occupied, housing has again become a source of income—not merely for the holders of building society share accounts, but for nearly ten million home owners too.

The gazumping boom marked the beginning of this new and critical phase in the history of home ownership, a phase in which under the political umbrella created by the *complaisant* housing policies of successive governments, falling industrial investment, high unemployment and a low rate of new construction now coincide with massive investment in housing and rapidly increasing house prices. To the extent that the new style of home ownership has converted the buying and selling of houses into a kind of alternative stock exchange activity,[1] through which investment which might rejuvenate industry is diverted instead into innumerable property transactions, it has created a new variant of the old housing problem. For a situation has arisen in which the buying and selling of houses, long identified in the public mind with the extension of home ownership, is now a business only tangentially related to that goal. There is in effect a conflict between the operations of the owner occupier market and the target of increased owner occupation which popularly legitimises it. Put in its

---

[1] An impression intensified by the growth of national and even international house selling agencies, such as the *National Network of Estate Agents*, which at the end of 1977 had 350 branch offices in the United Kingdom. Another such organisation, *Home Relocation*, "formed to coordinate the activities of the leading residential estate agents all over the country" has links with *All Points Relocation Service* in the United States, where similar central brokerage facilities have been in operation for a number of years.

simplest form this conflict means that the more often houses are bought and sold, the more difficult it becomes for a non owner-occupier to enter the owner-occupier market.

Today the intensification of investment and speculation in the private housing market has converted the old process of numerical growth, by which the number of home owners increased at the expense of other forms of tenure, into a pattern of wealth-creation in which a much less rapidly increasing number of privileged home owners grows progressively richer within a closed circuit of sales and resales priced beyond the reach of all who do not already own their own home. New construction can offer no answer to this, since it appears to be no more possible today than it was one hundred years ago to produce new houses at a low enough cost to meet unsubsidised demand. Nor indeed would any such innovation be welcomed if its consequence was to endanger the rising values which scarcity ensures.

When Anthony Crosland, the Labour Minister of the Environment, called in 1974 for a second "prefab" programme to combat the critical problems of homelessness and overcrowding in non-wealth-producing housing, his proposal was attacked by virtually every organisation connected with the housebuilding industry. The building societies, the builders, the architects, the producers of building materials, the trade associations, all opposed what they called "lower standards." In reality their objection was to the effect that any such influx of new building would have on the value of that which already existed; either reducing it or reducing the rate at which it was increasing. Such an eventuality might seem desirable at a time when rising housing costs are bewailed as though they were the result of some unavoidable natural catastrophe; but it is not. In the context of a growing reliance upon speculatively increased values, such a prospect has come to be alarming. In the words of the chief general manager of the Nationwide building society (explaining the refusal of all societies to lend on houses in deteriorating inner city areas) "If somebody buys a house for £10,000 and a year later it is worth only £9000 it will . . . be a personal tragedy for the man concerned."[1]

Presumably the loss of 80% of all share values between 1968

[1] Mr Leonard Williams, interviewed by John Young in *The Times* 16th December 1977.

and 1974 was a personal tragedy for many investors, but on the stock exchange it has always been regarded as part of the game. Only in the new world of the owner speculators are the rules set up in such a way that gains are inevitable and losses—even when they in no way affect the use-value of the dwelling itself—so uncommon that their meaning is no longer understood. As Peter Jay wrote in *Time* magazine,[1] before he began to see grounds for optimism in those very disasters he so capably analysed, "When ordinary, decent, sensible people are forced into a conflict between what they perceive to be their own private interest and what they probably accept are the interests of the country, there is no way in which they can put the two things together."

As Fig. 2 shows, the rate of completions of new houses for owner-occupation has been low since 1968 and, because of the large number of "recycled" mortgages in every year bears little relation to the fluctuating rate of issue of new mortgages by the building societies. In this respect the consultative arrangements established between government and societies in 1975 have had no effect whatever. The owner-occupier market could in theory operate with no new building at all, almost as it did during the Second World War; for the rate of addition achieved by the construction industry is negligible in relation to the total stock of marketable houses.

Since new construction must be ruled out as a major resource for the further expansion of home ownership, we are left with a situation in which enormous demand for the economic advantages of owner-occupation coexists with market conditions in which its satisfaction grows increasingly unlikely. According to current demographic projections the end of the crude housing shortage in England and Wales (there are already half a million more dwellings than households, excluding second homes) means the end of large-scale housing programmes. At the same time the end of sales out of private rental is imminent. If home ownership is to grow in the future at the same rate as it has grown in the past, it will no longer be able to do so in the same way.

The official answer to this predicament differs between the two major political parties. The Labour Party assumes that this dead

[1] *Time* magazine, European edition 30th September 1974, "Britain adrift in a deepening crisis of faith."

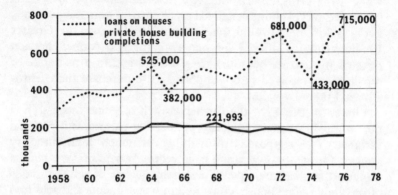

Fig. 2   Great Britain: private housebuilding completions (annual) plotted against Building Society loans on houses (annual). Completions: *Annual Abstract of Statistics;* loans on houses: Building Societies Association.

end can be interpreted as meaning that stability in tenure distribution has at last been reached. According to their own Housing Policy Review the next decade will see public-sector rental and owner-occupation cut private-sector rental to an irreducible rump constituting perhaps 8% of all dwellings by 1986. At the same time home ownership will have increased by a further 4 or 5% from 9.9 million dwellings to 11.9 million, stabilising at about 60% of the total stock—itself some two million dwellings larger. The public rental sector, taking care of all those unable to buy, no matter how intensely they desire to, will constitute the remaining third. There will be no substantial selling from public rental into private ownership.

The problem with such projections, no matter how closely they appear to follow the foreseeable population base for the formation of new households, is that they ignore the tremendous dynamic which has built up behind demand for home ownership and the manner in which it could be converted into purchasing power which would find no other target but the millions of potentially saleable houses in the public sector. As long ago as 1967 a survey conducted by the Opinion Research Centre suggested that owner-occupation was the aspiration of 43% of council tenants, while 1977 press reports inferred that an unpublished NEDC sponsored survey shows a national preference for ownership of 70% rising to 80% in the younger age groups. In May 1977 the Greater London Council offered for sale two hundred council houses, rejected by tenants because they were old and in a bad state of repair. They received 11,000 applications to purchase and eventually sold them by ballot.

Viewed in this light the further growth of home ownership is not so much a demographically predictable pattern as a political variable. The supposed unsuitability of much local-authority housing for owner-occupation is no more likely to prove a serious obstacle than was the equally unsuitable nature of the thousands of privately rented houses converted into apartments and sold into owner-occupation over the last fifty years. Where the economic advantages are commensurate, the ingenuity deployed will be equal to the occasion.

The posture of the Conservative Party in relation to home ownership is thus a critical factor—perhaps in relation to its own political future as much as to the future of home ownership. By throwing open five million council tenancies to purchase they might begin another era of growth as rapid and spectacular as that of the last quarter century. But the economic and social consequences of such an action would be incalculable, for as we have seen home ownership is already a massive and complex phenomenon, with implications and consequences extending into almost every area of modern life.

For the owner-occupiers, who already own 55% of the stock in an electorally sound if ethically suspect company, the term "housing crisis" has no real meaning. And yet crisis is the right word to describe the predicament of home ownership in the last quarter of the 20th century. The present "Pretty good arrangement" (to use the title of a 1975 building societies promotional film) can neither be allowed to continue without growing social and economic inequality, nor can it easily be arrested without serious economic and political complications. Owner-occupiers are too numerous and too innocent to be villainised in the manner of the "wicked" landlord.

Bibliography

Addison, P. *The Road to 1945: British Politics and the Second World War* Jonathan Cape 1975

Berry, F. *Housing: The Great British Failure* Knight 1974

Clarke, C. and G. T. Jones *The Demand for Housing* Centre for Environmental Studies 1971

Clay, H. *Economics for the General Reader* Macmillan 1916

Cleary, E. J. *The Building Society Movement* Elek 1965

Donnison, D. V. *The Government of Housing* Pelican 1967

Dow, J. C. R. *The Management of the British Economy 1945–60* Cambridge University Press 1970

Elmer Wood, E. *Recent Trends in American Housing* New York 1931

Engels, F. *The Origin of the Family, Private Property, and the State* London 1884

England, K. M. (editor) *Housing: A Citizen's Guide to the Problem* Chatto & Windus 1931

Facts and Figures: a Quarterly Bulletin of Statistics and Background Commentary on Housing and Housing Finance The Building Societies' Association

Flinn, M. W. *British Population Growth 1700–1850* Studies in Economic History, Macmillan 1970

Gray, H. *The Cost of Council Housing* Institute of Economic Affairs 1968

Greve, J. *Private Landlords in England* Occasional Papers on Social Administration No 16, Bell 1965

Halsey, A. H. *Trends in British Society since 1900* Macmillan 1972

Handbook: Facts and Figures for Socialists Labour Party Research Department 1951

Hole, W. V. and M. T. Pountney *Trends in Population, Housing and Occupancy Rates 1861–1961* Department of the Environmental/Building Research Station, HMSO 1971

Housing and Construction Statistics (quarterly) Department of the Environment, HMSO

Housing Policy: a Consultative Document Cmnd 6851, HMSO 1977

Housing Policy Review: Technical Volumes I–III HMSO 1977

Hutchison, K. *The Decline and Fall of British Capitalism* Cape 1951

Inequality in Britain Today Labour Party Research Department 1977

Kirkman Gray, B. *A History of English Philanthropy* London 1905 (reprinted Cass 1967)

Macfarlane, L. J. *Issues in British Politics since 1945* Longman 1975

Madge, J. (editor) *Tomorrow's Houses* Pilot 1946

Marriott, O. *The Property Boom* Hamish Hamilton 1967

McAllister, G. and E. G. McAllister *Town and Country Planning* Faber 1941

Milward, A. S. *The Economic Effects of Two World Wars on Britain* Macmillan 1970

Methods of Encouraging Home Ownership: a Preliminary International Survey The Housing Research Foundation 1970

National Income and Expenditure 1966–76 Central Statistical Office 1976

The National Plan Cmnd 2764, HMSO 1965

Price, S. J. *Building Societies: Their Origin and History* Franey 1958

The Renter Prospects: A Survey of Households Who Rent But Could Afford To Buy The Housing Research Foundation 1971

Soules, G. *The Housing Crisis: Causes, Effects, Solutions* Soules (Vancouver) 1976

Trevelyan, G. M. *British History in the Nineteenth Century and After (1782–1919)* Longman 1937

Tucker, J. *Honourable Estates* Gollancz 1966

Woodforde, J. *The Truth about Cottages* Routledge, Kegan Paul 1969

Whittick, A. *The Small House: Today and Tomorrow* Leonard Hill 1947

Index